PUPIL
EVALUATION
IN THE CLASSROOM

An All Level Guide
to Practice

Douglas M. Brooks
David W. Van Cleaf

Center for Professional Teacher Education
University of Texas at Arlington

UNIVERSITY
PRESS OF
AMERICA

LANHAM • NEW YORK • LONDON

Copyright © 1982 by

University Press of America,™ Inc.

4720 Boston Way
Lanham, MD 20706

3 Henrietta Street
London WC2E 8LU England

Library of Congress Cataloging in Publication Data

Brooks, Douglas M.
   Pupil evaluation in the classroom.

   1. Students, Rating of. I. Van Cleaf, David W. II.
Title.
LB1117.B67   1982   371.2'7   82–13650
ISBN 0–8191–2736–1
ISBN 0–8191–2737–X (pbk.)

All University Press of America books are produced on acid-free
paper which exceeds the minimum standards set by the National
Historical Publications and Records Commission.

Preface

The primary objective of this manuscript is to provide beginning and practicing teachers with specific, realistic and grade level appropriate strategies for evaluating pupil academic and social behavior. We deliberately avoided the overuse of technical vocabulary that might require pages of explanation. The approaches and strategies we have suggested have been field tested. Our combined classroom experience, coupled with our training, has only heightened our commitment to evaluation procedures that take into account child development, academic and social self concept, and measurement practices. While standard test and measurement texts address more topics than we have in this text, we feel the content we have included will provide the reader with common sense skill awareness. We want, more than anything, for the reader to be a successful classroom teacher. We hope this manuscript increases the probability of a successful classroom experience.

TABLE OF CONTENTS

TABLE OF CONTENTS

TABLE OF CONTENTS

TABLE OF CONTENTS

TABLE OF CONTENTS

CHAPTER 1

THE VOCABULARY OF A PHILOSOPHY OF EVALUATION

"The most important [reason for] a test is to do it well because you get good grades on your report cards and your parents would be proud to hear you've done good on your tests." - Jessica (4th Grade)

Evaluation is so much a part of classroom instruction that we rarely question the process. Teachers require, construct, administer and score classroom tests so naturally you might think there was a gene for it. To test is so simple: make the test about two pages; have it one hundred total points; never say what is going to be on the test; administer it on Fridays; and hand it back on Mondays. This sequence occurs so frequently that altering the process would seem unthinkable. If the evaluation process was changed, then it just would not be classroom testing. It would be something foreign to schooling as we know it. In the absence of any formal training, new teachers are likely to administer tests just as they had been administered to them. What could be more natural?

So what about you? If the way you were tested in schools seemed OK, maybe you had better not read any further. We may raise some questions that could frighten you. For the rest of you, suppose that not all your teachers thought about what they were doing. Maybe they tested because it seemed natural. What if you had some problems with the way you were evaluated in school? What are you likely to do when you have the responsibility to test? Maybe a good place to start is to consider your philosophy of evaluation.

A philosophy can be a very comforting thing. A philosophy will help you make decisions and it will help you organize yourself. It also will help you examine and evaluate conflicting points of view. And, it might just help you stop doing what seems natural. There is no doubt that if you think about why we evaluate in schools and consider the appropriate methods for each type of evaluation, you will be able to test more effectively.

WHAT IS GOING TO BE EVALUATED?

A common source of confusion in classroom testing is the object of the evaluation. Common objects of evaluation are people, processes, and products. These three evaluation objects are forever getting confused in the classroom. In most cases you will be evaluating a product. This product may be a term paper, an art project, a chapter test or a book report. The important thing to remember is that if you have decided to evaluate a product, you must insure that this is all you evaluate. A teacher comment like, "It isn't that I don't like you, the problem is that I don't like what you're doing", demonstrates the fine line between product and person evaluation.

I was very interested in industrial arts as a junior high student. My first woodworking project was a cherry salad bowl. I glued the pieces together, shaped the bowl on a wood lathe and finished it with a satin varnish. I worked very hard on the bowl and received a grade of 90 for my efforts. I have always wondered what a 100 bowl would have looked like? Anyway, my next project was a toothbrush holder. This project was much easier and I had it built and finished in a week. I received an 80 on the toothbrush holder. When I asked why I had received a lower grade,' my shop teacher replied that I had not worked as long on the toothbrush holder and had not put in as much work on it. I nodded my head and left. Actually, the toothbrush holder more closely approximated a toothbrush holder than the bowl did a bowl. That did not seem to matter. It turned out that what was being evaluated was the process and the person, not the product.

2

The evaluation of math work or term papers is another place where product and process evaluation should be separated, but generally are not. It may be more important for a student to understand how to do a term paper or how to do a math problem than to be overly concerned with the end product. This would seem to be common sense during the early stages of a learning experience. Maybe math teachers should pay more attention to process evaluation than the right answer. That is, math teachers should check students' work to determine their understanding of the steps rather than evaluate the percent of problems correctly completed. When you consider the number of term papers that are copied, sold, or stolen and handed in for grading, it is not hard to figure out that the emphasis has been on the product evaluation and not process evaluation.

In many areas of classroom instruction and in many disciplines, a separate type of evaluation for process would help to identify errors that contribute to poor products. The question to ask yourself is, "Is there a process I should be evaluating independent of the product I will be evaluating?" If there is a process to be evaluated, separate it from the product evaluation and assign separate grades.

WHAT IS THE REASON FOR YOUR EVALUATION?

Evaluation in schools is generally for the purpose of selection, placement or treatment. Selection decisions are accept or reject decisions. Selection decisions tend to be final in nature. A classroom test may be used to select the high achievers from the low achievers. If classroom tests serve any purpose in most cases it seems to be this type of selection. Classroom grades become semester grades, which then become semester averages, which then become criteria for selection into college or other vocational outlets. We somehow seem to always be selecting the bright from the disadvantaged. You cannot join

3

an academic organization without specific academic credentials. Therefore, selection type evaluations tend to dominate classroom instruction.

Testing for placement occurs frequently in reading and mathematics. Placement decisions often follow from selection decisions. For example, a student may get placed in the high reading group. However, the usual decision is based on accumulated classroom grades, independent of more objective evaluation techniques. Interestingly enough, the very bright and the less successful students experience the majority of selection and placement evaluations.

But when do we use evaluation in schools for treatment purposes? Examine the word treatment when it is used in a medical sense. If a patient is to be treated, the physician first must know what the patient has or does not have wrong with him. The first evaluation is diagnostic, not final. The first evaluation is a starting point, or guide to treatment. The treatment itself is designed to make the patient well - as well as every other healthy patient. The physician's motto is not "some better than others", but "all equally healthy." The critical question is, "How do classroom tests usually function?"

The traditional testing model in operation in the majority of classrooms supports the selection position, not the treatment position. The test scores are used to decide who will receive "A's" and who will receive "F's". If you need "F's", you have to have some method for deciding who gets them. If you need a valedictorian, what better way to get one than to give a summative, one time only test with irreversible grades that accumulate to the disadvantage of the less gifted. We rely too heavily on selection as a motivation for testing. The motivation for testing should be treatment. Diagnostic tests could be given at the beginning of every unit. Formative tests should be given to see if the students

4

are acquiring instructional objectives. Teachers can administer remedial instruction if necessary following the evaluation. The summative tests (end of unit) could occur when the pupil is ready to demonstrate mastery or near mastery. This series of evaluations represents a program of evaluation designed to produce mastery, not just assess mastery.

WHEN DO YOU WANT TO HAVE INFORMATION?

The traditional time for information gathering is on Friday. Have the students learned what I expected? The Friday testing syndrome implies that testing may not be part of instruction, but rather a procedure separate from instruction. Does Friday testing tell the teacher whether the pupils have learned what has been presented? How do you know you taught them anything if you only test at the end of the unit? This would be like a doctor testing all the patients discharged from the hospital and taking personal credit for making them well. If you only want information at the end, then test at the end. If you want to use classroom tests to select for "A's" and "F's", first you need students who are at different achievement levels. Secondly, instruct all of them with the same method and, finally, administer a summative test on Friday. Then you will get the differences you seek.

But, if you are going to view your instruction as a treatment designed to make them all equally competent, then you need information before you begin teaching and at various points during your instruction. A pretest will give you information prior to instruction. The pretest should indicate each student's initial entering knowledge level. You can organize your Tuesday instruction from the information you collected with the pretest. The instructional options then become numerous. You can lightly touch or eliminate the information pupils already know. You could let students who already know the

5

material help those who do not know it as well.

You might like to know if anybody is learning anything toward the middle of the week. Why not give a formative test to see if your students are learning? The test will tell you and the pupils what they have not mastered. The formative information could help you organize your Thursday instruction. You might want to review what has been particularly difficult to master. The end result of this testing and adjusting of instruction is that you are likely to minimize individual differences in summative performance. The only grade that counts is the summative one. The two prior evaluations are designed to help the student and the teacher. Teachers need to be willing to ask for and collect data in order to enhance instruction.

HOW DO YOU WANT TO ASSIGN GRADES?

When we think about assigning grades the term that frequently comes to mind is comparison. Test grades should reflect skill attainment relative to some standard. The standard of comparison can take the form of a self-referenced standard, a norm-referenced standard, or a criterion-referenced standard. Each standard supports a particular motive for evaluation.

The self-referenced method of grade assignment requires a comparison of the student's test score with his or her previous score on an equivalent form of the same test. If the second score is higher, then the pupil has acquired information from the instructional process. Self-referenced grade assessment requires a pretest/posttest examination schedule. The teacher must know what the student already knows in order to assign a grade based on growth. Forty points of growth might be an "A", thrity points a "B", twenty points a "C", etc. Once baseline data is obtained, the teachers can make any kind of contractual agreement they want with the student.

6

The only requisite for this type of evaluation is that the pretest and posttest maintain essentially the same form. For example, a pretest essay should be judged by the same criteria as a posttest essay.

A norm-referenced method of comparison requires grade assignment through comparison with the norm group. Norm-referenced comparisons involve competition for the scarce resources of high grades. Norm-referenced comparisons are based on the premise that regardless of how well everyone does, some will do better than others. Skill attainment becomes less important than establishing the norm group to which you will be compared. Norm-referenced strategies for grade assignment serve the selection rationale very well. Normative comparisons discriminate between the top, middle and bottom. There will always be a top and there will always be a bottom in the normative grade distribution. If you need to create a top, norm-reference your scores.

A criterion-referenced method of grade assignment requires comparison of a pupil's performance with a predetemined level of performance. Grade assignment follows the demonstration of competence or mastery at the criterion level of choice. For example, when you have spelled all ten words correctly, you may go on to the next spelling lesson. When you can work five of the seven math problems correctly, you may go on to the next page. The criterion-referenced method of grade assignment requires that the teacher decide in advance what is an acceptable level of performance. Criterion-referenced measurement is independent of the performance of the peer group or class. Grades are assessed based on a pupil's ability to achieve the predetermined criteria.

Summatively, if a student spells eight out of ten spelling words correctly, he could potentially receive three different grades, depending on the selected method of grade assignment. He might receive a "F" if everyone else spelled all ten words correctly. He could receive a "B" if on the pretest he agreed to spell all the words on the posttest correctly for an "A". He could receive an "A", if the teacher had decided that a competence level of 8 out of 10 was required for an "A". The same number of words have been spelled correctly, but three different grades can be assigned. How fair would it be if three sixth grade teachers used a different method to evaluate a spelling test? All three pupils have spelled 8 out of 10 words, but the grades they received could range from "A" to "F".

WHAT IS THE INTENT OF YOUR GRADING SYSTEM?

If your intent is to determine deviation from average class performance or compare one pupil with a norm group, then a norm-referenced style of grade assignment would be appropriate. When grades are curved the scores are expressed as deviations from the arithmetic average. If the mean is high or low, it does not matter. This method will always produce a fixed percentage of "A's" and "F's".

If your intent is to assess mastery or to compare a pupil's performance with a predetermined level of competence then a criterion-referenced style of grade assignment would be appropriate. The mastery comparison is independent of group performance; it allows you to evaluate individual task mastery.

WHY DID YOU DECIDE TO TEACH SCHOOL?

The different questions that have been raised in this chapter are meant to introduce a vocabulary that should help you formulate a philosophy of evaluation. Questions like "What are you going to evaluate?", "Why are you evaluating?", "When do you want the information?", and "How do you want to assign grades?" all depend on

8

the intent of your evaluation. If the intent of your evaluation is estimate deviation from average group performance, then words like selection, placement, summative and norm-referenced should be part of your evaluation philosophy. If the intent of your evaluation content is mastery, then words like treatment, pretest, formative, self-referenced, and norm-referenced should be part of your evaluation vocabulary.

Once you have determined intent, the rest is simply a matter of organizing the pieces. There is, however, one question that overshadows the others. That question is the one that began this section. Why did you decide to teach school? Did you decide to teach school so you could help the first grade teacher decide who should be a second grader? Did you decide to teach school so you could show the college admissions people who would be the best applicants? Did you decide to teach school so Phi Beta Kappa would not make a mistake in selecting a member? Do you get our point? For as long as we have been teaching school, people have implied that we should improve instruction to facilitate content mastery, yet we have systematically participated in grading systems that are so future oriented that they totally ignore the present. We have heard administrators say that we give too many "A's" as if it were impossible to organize instruction in such a manner that pupils earn the "A's" they receive. We have seen curious, motivated learners turn on each other like a pack of starving wolves when the teacher announces that he or she only allows a fixed number of "A's". Proclamations of this type are usually expressed as a defense of standards. We have always wanted to ask whose standards? The critics behave as if the school system is something independent of the people in it.

When we first taught school we began evaluating as we had been evaluated. We gave Friday tests, assigned "A's" and "F's", averaged grades,

9

and filled out grade reports. We eventually
realized that we were participating in a process
that seemed to be designed for the elite, the
skilled, the privileged. The same students suc-
ceeded every week. The same students failed.
Instruction was emphasized, but something was
lacking. Our tests were breaking the spirits of
our students. We were pitting them against one
another, but did not know why. It all seemed so
natural. We even marked incorrect responses with
a traditional red pen.

A group of low sixth grade math students
helped alter our philosophy of evaluation. They
were the walking wounded. Each felt they would
never see an "A" because the high group always
received the "A's". Motivation to learn was nonexistent. There was nothing to lose, so we
decided that rather than try to determine who the
best of the worst were, we would try to treat all
of them at their individual ability levels. The
evaluation system that emerged was one of encouragement and mastery. Each student was treated
according to his or her need in the context of a
thirty student class. Each student began to progress and master the tasks of elementary math.
Once they were not competing with each other they
could focus on content mastery, and they actually
began to enjoy the idea of coming to math class.

If you worry less about the next year and
more about this year, then next year will take
care of itself. We can think of nothing more
foolish than having an evaluation style that
cripples most students today, so that a few may
run tomorrow.

You entered teaching to make a difference
in the lives of children. The difference you
make will be based on what you teach them. If
they refuse to learn because your philosophy of
evaluation is crippling, are you doing your job?
It is time to learn. You entered teaching to
educate children. Ideally you would like each of

your students to fulfill their potential. Individual potential can be realized if attention is paid to an evaluation philosophy that positively affects your classroom evaluation practices.

SUGGESTED READINGS

Schultz, Richard E. "The Role of Measurement in Education: Servant, Soulmate, Stoolpigeon, Statesman, Scapegoat, All of the Above, and/or None of the Above." Journal of Educational Measurement 8, No. 3 (Fall, 1971).

Buchwald, A.M. "Values and the Use of Tests." Journal of Consulting Psychology, 1965, 29, 49-54.

Wittrock, M.C. and David E. Wiley (eds.): The Evaluation of Instructional Issues and Problems, Holt Rinehart and Winston, Inc. New York: 1970.

Holt, John. The Underachieving School. Dell Publishing Company, New York: 1969.

Slater, Philip. The Pursuit of Loneliness: American Culture at the Breaking Point. Becon Press, Boston: 1971.

Perkinson, H. J. The Imperfect Panacea: American Faith in Education: 1865-1965. Random House: 1968.

11

CHAPTER 2

ANALYZING CONTENT FOR EFFECTIVE EVALUATION

"We never know what we are expected
to know. The lectures don't help
us with the tests. The tests don't
have anything to do with the book or
the lectures. The whole thing seems
to be put together to torture me."
-Anson (college freshman)

In theory, agreement between selected
instructional objectives and appropriate curriculum materials can happen. Once instructional
objectives are identified by the teacher, principal, district or community, appropriate curriculum materials can be selected and purchased.
Occassionally, such materials include suggested
test items. In practice, a less than perfect
match between instructional objectives, curriculum materials and test items is what usually
occurs. A text book is adopted by the school
district and the books are given to teachers during the first week of in-service. The teacher is
encouraged to cover as much of the text or texts
as possible in one hundred and eighty school
days. The teacher relies on the lecture method
of instruction and then constructs their own
tests.

Classroom teachers tend to rely on textbooks as a major source for instructional goals,
therefore we hope to help the classroom teacher
cope with reality. We propose a practical four
step model for developing a fair classroom test.
We start with the standard text book. A visual
presentation of our model is presented in Figure
1.

Figure 1

Four Step Model for Instructional Evaluation

Step I	Step II	Step III	Step IV
Analysis of Text- book Content	Sequencing Instruc- tional Goals	Selection of Appro- priate Instruc- tional Methodology	Selection of Appro- priate Test- Items

---

ANALYZING THE STANDARD TEXT

Classroom textbooks begin as outlines in the minds of the authors. The author is gen- erally regarded as someone who "knows the field". The author determines the grade level of the pro- posed test, surveys other texts which may be regarded as competitors and begins the lengthy process of organizing and sequencing important content. The content is most often presented in a linear fashion from least complex and most basic to most complex and abstract.

A casual survey of many middle school and secondary level textbooks reveals the similari- ties important to careful analysis of the text- books. The authors begin by organizing the total content to be presented into cognitive units called chapters. Each chapter includes the author's goals. Each chapter includes the intro- duction of new knowledge, may apply prior know- ledge, or preview knowledge to be presented in later chapters. A first level of analysis begins with the question "What are the goals of the text as defined by the titles of the chapters?" For example, an eighth grade math text might contain the general content goals suggested in Figure 2.

Figure 2

Math Text General Content Goals

CHAPTER	1.	Sentencing and Variables
CHAPTER	2.	Reasoning Patterns
CHAPTER	3.	Integer Systems
CHAPTER	4.	Rational Numbers
CHAPTER	5.	Applying Rational Numbers
CHAPTER	6.	Approximations
CHAPTER	7.	Review
CHAPTER	8.	Circles
CHAPTER	9.	Real Numbers
CHAPTER	10.	Area
CHAPTER	11.	Statistics
CHAPTER	12.	Probability
CHAPTER	13.	Geometry

This visual is an example of a general content analysis of the textbook. This level of analysis will outline the years general instructional content. Figure 2 is probably very much like the original text outline as visualized by the authors. Any standard text can be diagrammed in such a manner.

The next step in text analysis is to determine the specific content goals of individual chapters. This level of analysis will provide the teacher with an understanding of the author's instructional goals within a specific chapter. Careful content analysis may also provide a guide to the selection of appropriate instructional methods. Robert Gagne (1965) has developed and presented a schemata which describes levels of learning. He identified eight different types or levels of learning. The levels presented in Figure 3, can be used as an organizer for the goal analysis of chapter content.

15

Figure 3

Gagne's Eight Types of Learning

---

1. Signal learning. The student is asked to
    respond in a general manner to a sig-
    nal. Example: A pupil lines up for
    attendance when the P.E. teacher blows
    a whistle.

2. Stimulus-response learning. The student
    learns a precise response to a speci-
    fic stimulus. Example: Pronouncing
    sounds of the alphabet.

3. Motor chaining. The student learns a series
    of stimulus response behaviors.

4. Verbal association. The student learns verbal
    sequences. Example: Being able to
    remember the words to a song.

5. Discrimination learning. The student learns
    to discriminate between objects or
    sounds. Example: Learning that port
    is left and starboard is right.

6. Concept learning. The student makes a common
    response to objects which are different
    but share one attribute unique to a
    class. Example: A student recognizes
    that there are many types of monopolies
    but all monopolies share the same char-
    acteristics.

7. Rule learning. The student learns application
    of rules in differing contexts. Exam-
    ple: The student applies honesty is
    the best policy at home and during
    visits to friends.

8. Problem solving. The learner combines rules to
    solve problems. Example: Working   -
    geometry proofs to demonstrate theorems.

Gagne's eight levels may be used as organizers for analysis of content, organization of instruction, and the construction of classroom tests. The two most important questions to ask in an analysis of chapter content are: (1) Within which of Gagne's levels of learning does the content of the chapter fall? (2) What is the nature of substance of the content? The actual questioning process requires that you ask such questions as, "Does the chapter ask the student to associate one term with another?", and "Does the chapter ask the student to learn a process, discriminate between terms, introduce new concepts or rules, or are they asked to solve any problems or transfer information"?

Figure 4

Relationship Between Levels of Learning
and Content Goals

Level of learning	Content
Signal learning	Recognition of states on map
Stimulus response	Saying the preamble
Motor chaining	Writing an amendment
Verbal associations	Learning letters of the alphabet
Discrimination learning	Difference between the 13th and 14th amendments
Concept learning	Amendment, President, Congress
Problem solving	Conditions that lead to war and present conditions

The format of textbooks can assist the teacher in content analysis. Key concepts or terms often appear in italics. Discriminations and associations are highlighted in graphs, drawings, pictures or explanations. Questions at the end of chapters will provide clues to the author's instructional goals.

This content analysis reduces the storyline of the chapter to the skeletal content. It is the skeletal content that is important in achievement testing. The reality of public school is that many processes, associations, discriminations, concepts and problem solving goals are introduced. It seems common sense that an analysis process that helps organize goals and instruction can facilitate learning. Figure 5 is an example of a list of instructional goals expressed in a skeletal/low inference format. This format may serve as a guide to both the instructor and the student as they prepare for instruction and learning.

Figure 5

Low Inference Goals for Instructional
Unit Planning

---

1. Charter- a piece of paper given by the King telling what rights the person had and the location of the land

2. Know what the passengers from England hoped to find in North America. Land, jobs, religious freedom; Passengers - LJRF

3. Jamestown - first successful English settlement in North America

4. King James I - Jamestown

5. Location of settlers - rivers, oceans and plains (rop)

(Figure 5 - Continued)

6. Name and locate the 13 colonies on the provided map.

1.	New Hampshire	8.	South Carolina
2.	New Jersey	9.	Georgia
3.	New York	10.	Delaware
4.	Rhode Island	11.	Pennsylvania
5.	Connecticut	12.	Massachusetts
6.	Virginia	13.	Maryland
7.	North Carolina		

7. Merchants - trading

8. Indentured Servant - exchanged passage for a
   period of work

9. Error of Jamestown - searched for gold

10. John Smith Rule - work in order to get food

11. Founders of New York - Dutch

12. Unmarried girls wanted to come to North
    American to find husbands

13. Know that Plymouth and London or Virgina Com-
    panies were the two companies that started the
    colonies

14. Mayflower - Plymouth in 1620

15. England's government helped solve the working
    shortage in America by sending orphans,
    prisoners of war and criminals to America

The underlining in goals 1-5 represent potential mnemonic devices that could aid the teacher
and pupil in recalling the answers to test questions.

19

SEQUENCING INSTRUCTIONAL GOALS

Content goals should be expressed in instructional goal terminology. These instructional goals should be sequentially presented with the more basic or fundamental objectives taught first and more complex problem solving objectives taught last. Figure 6 presents a visual example of sequencing instructional goals.

Figure 6

Sequencing Instructional Goals

Lower Level Goals	Higher Level Goals
1. List the thirteen colonies	1. Why did the colony at Jamestown struggle for survival?
2. Define charter	
3. Define merchants	2. Why did the colonies have trouble uniting?
4. Who was John Smith?	
	3. How would you set up a new colony?

A well stated instructional goal should be student-oriented, describe a learning outcome in observable terms, suggest a context for demonstrating proficiency and include criteria for judging success. Unlike traditional lesson plans which merely identify the pages that will be covered on a particular day, a well written instructional goal can emerge easily from a content analysis of the text, can direct the pupil to the task of what is to be learned, and can guide the instructional method of the teacher. Lesson plans that are not goal specific, interfere with effective instruction and pupil mastery.

SELECTING APPROPRIATE INSTRUCTIONAL METHODS

Traditional reliance on the lecture method of classroom instruction has only recently been seriously challenged by teaching machines, individually guided instruction, alternative learning environments and inquiry methods. The lecture method has continued to weather the assaults of more sophisticated instructional styles because it continues to be the best strategy for directing the learning task with thirty students in a fifty minute time frame with maximum classroom control. Where educators have errored is in their all or nothing approach to educational innovation. They seem to see each new technique or gimmick as the innovation that will revolutionize children's learning. A much more realistic approach would be to consider each innovation as potentially useful in facilitating a particular level of learning. Figure 7 presents a possible organization schemata for synchronizing instructional method with instructional objectives.

Figure 7

The Relationship Between Goal Level and
Instructional Method

A. memorization
1. teacher introduction
2. private practice
3. peer teaching
4. opportunities to test for mastery

B. application
1. transfer assignments
2. projects
3. in class activities
4. question and answer type lessons
5. association with current events

C. problem solving
1. simulations
2. hypothesis generation activities
3. group jig sawing methodology
4. inductive teaching methods

SELECTING THE APPROPRIATE TEST ITEM

The selection of appropriate test items is the final step in developing a useful and fair evaluation program. Testing is part of teaching, not something independent of teaching. Your classroom tests should reflect your content, instructional goals and instructional methodology. Specific types of test items are designed to test particular levels of content and instruction. The advantages and disadvantages of each item type are discussed here as well as their relationship to specific levels of content.

Matching questions, true-false questions, alternative response questions and multiple choice questions are designed to measure simple learning outcomes (ie., names and dates, states and capitals, etc.). Item types of this sort are useful tools for evaluating lower level instructional goals. They form the major portion of many classroom tests. These items are often the most poorly written test items.

Fill-in-the blank, defining terms and short answer item types constitute a higher level of testing. Comprehension, discrimination, and application of instructional goals are readily tested with these test item types. These test item types commonly require recall and not just recognition type responses. The pupil is required to provide the answer, not just decide from choices provided in the question.

Extended and restricted essay questions can be used to assess recall of related facts or encourage the student o analyze, synthesize and/or problem solve. Discrimination, analysis, synthesis and evaluation level instructional goals are appropriately evaluated with essay item types. While essay item types are fairly easy to compose they are extremely difficult to objectively grade. Figure 8 provides a visual display of the relationship between levels of learning and test item types.

22

Figure 8

Relationship Between Levels of Learning
and Test Item Type

Level of learning	Item type
signal learning stimulus response motor chaining	alternate response multiple choice/fill-in- the-blank, matching
verbal association discrimination	alternate response true-false items
comprehension application concept learning	short answer short answer, essay definition and explanation
analysis problem solving synthesis evaluation	restricted essay structured essay extended essay extended essay

The four step model that we have suggested
for developing a classroom test is admittedly a
conservative approach to organizing for instruction and evaluation. Similarly, the premise that
you should initially accept the instructional
content presented by the textbook author is also
conservative. Each of us would like to think
that we have the subject matter training to
determine instructional objectives and then adapt
the appropriate materials. But remember reality,
classroom testing has an abysmal reputation.
Teachers are, in fact, given state adopted texts,
and expected to teach from those materials. To
ignore school prescribed curriculum materials is
an invitation to problems.

23

So which is the worst crime, to prepare a teacher for a world that does not exist or prepare a teacher for a world that, while imperfect, will most certainly be there Monday. We believe that teachers need success in schools. We believe that success is determined in part by realistic, fair, and purposeful classroom evaluation. Any method or model that will better serve the interests of fair evaluation is worth the price of an initially conservative design.

References

Gagne, R. M. "The Analysis of Instructional Objectives for the Design of Instruction," W. R. Glasser (ed), Teaching Machines and Programmed Learning, II: Data and Directives, NEA, Washington, D. C. 1965

Bloom, Benjamin S. (ed) Toxonomy of Educational Objectives, Handbook I. The Cognitive Domain, David McKay Company, Inc. New York, 1956.

Tenbrink, T. D. Evaluation: a practical guide for teacher. McGraw-Hill Book Company, New York: 1974.

CHAPTER 3

TEST PLANNING AND TEST ITEM CONSTRUCTION

> "Some of my teachers seem to get a sadistic kind of pleasure out of making up test questions that are confusing. It seems like part of the game is figuring out how to make things more difficult than they really are". -Jonathan (high school junior).

Authors and teachers may disagree on some matters of format, but most will agree that there are some common sense considerations that any teacher should attend to in constructing a classroom test. We will offer ten guidelines that we feel may help you to earn a reputation as a fair classroom test maker. When you consider that the number one source of anxiety among pupils is performance on tests, it should come as no surprise that the teacher with the reputation for good tests is usually the teacher with fewer classroom management problems.

TEN GUIDELINES FOR TEST PLANNING

Testing Should be Considered a Part of Instruction

The perception many teachers have and most students have is that testing is not part of instruction. This perception has developed, in part, because of the habits developed around the testing act. We have a tendency to test on Fridays. The threat of tests is sometimes used as a motivator. Teachers sometimes don't consider the test as an opportunity to analyze the effectiveness of their teaching. Nor do they view testing as another instructional medium for the student. Formative evaluations, for example can be very useful diagnostic tools. The teacher has the opportunity to see what the students have not mastered. This information can help structure the content of the next day's lesson. Students also have a chance to see what they have yet to learn.

Test Content Should Reflect Instructional Content

The content of a test should be taken from the subject matter presented during instruction, and the instructional content should follow from the selected instructional objectives. A significant cause of bad testing is test content or questions that are based on information that has never been addressed during instruction; such as test items from footnotes or test items from other text sources. Teachers will sometimes use text publishers' tests. They have them typed up and run off without checking to be sure all the test items reflect content covered in class. Content that was not taught in class may suddenly appear on the test. Trick questions or extra point questions from other chapters take advantage of the pupil who has not anticipated trick questions or supplemental content. A test over Chapter 3 should come from your class notes, or what was presented in the text, not from the author's test questions or a quick review of the chapter by the teacher the night before the day of the test. Therefore, teachers must ensure that test questions reflect instructional goals. Not only is this approach instructionally appropriate, it is the easiest way to organize instruction and testing.

Test Emphasis Should Reflect Instructional Emphasis

The guiding principle in this statement should be obvious. If you spend three days on the theme of an Edgar Allen Poe story, then the unit test items should cover the theme of Edgar Allen Poe's story equally as thoroughly. The percentage of instructional time should suggest the percentage of test questions included on the test. Nothing is more unfair than misleading a student on the possible emphasis of test content.

A teacher may spend no time on a topic, thus it would be unfair to allow that topic to dominate the test. Classroom instruction should guide pupil preparation for tests. Yet knowing this, some teachers will purposely emphasize with test items, content that was not even hinted at during instruction. A good idea for highlighting the importance of particular test questions is to type the number of points per item on each sub-section of the test, ie. matching (20 pts.), essay (10 pts.). Point emphasis should also reflect instructional empahsis. More points can be given to the content that had more emphasis placed on it during instruction.

Test Length Should Allow All Students to Complete the Test

If alloted test time results in imcomplete exams, then test scores are not an accurate measure of achievement. Some examinations are designed as speed tests, but we do not think classroom tests should reflect this objective. As the time shortens for test completion, students who are less confident about their ability will begin to rush. As they rush, they may not read as carefully as they do when they are under less stress. These same students may start guessing, even on questions they may know.

Perhaps the most unfortunate consequence of all is the fact that these same students are the ones that usually receive the lower grades. A long test with insufficient time for completion gives a clear advantage to the students who least need the advantage. Classroom tests should provide equal opportunity to demonstrate mastery. Teachers should not feel self-conscious because some students finish early in the period. This is the natural way of things in heterogeneous classrooms. The less gifted should not suffer in order that the more gifted should feel challenged. Remember, your job is to teach all students, not just those who happen to be bright.

27

Test Directions Should be Clear and Concise

Nothing is more frustrating to a student taking a test than confusing directions. The student may be eager to demonstrate mastery. Their proficiency may be threatened by incomprehensible directions. Your directions should be simply stated and they should preface each segment of the test or new item type. We favor the use of short complete sentences that leave nothing to the imagination. The student who is nervous or anxious about performance because of a history of poor grades will be the first to misread or misinterpret the directions. If your directions are oral, the more nervous student will not listen or be paying attention. If you forget or change a direction, write it on the board or an overhead projector.

Test Directions and Questions Should be Readable

The vocabulary of test directions and test items should be at least two grade levels below the reading level of your better students. Keep it simple. It is not unusual to have a wide range of reading ability within an average 9th grade class. A student might do very well on a test when it is read to him, but cannot perform on it when he must read it by himself. Directions and questions that the student can read will eliminate this common mistake as a potential source of error. The student should have every advantage to show his or her best work and not have it diminished by difficult test vocabulary.

Sequence Test Items

The sequencing of test items can improve performance on classroom tests. Begin the test with simple true-false questions. These questions provide an excellent warm-up for higher level questions. Additionally, matching, alternative response, and multiple choice questions are considered recognition type questions and should be positioned in the first part of the test. Recall type questions, like fill-in-the-blank and short answer, commonly follow recognition, questions. Essay questions, considered more difficult, should be located toward the end of the test. If the essay questions are located at the beginning of the test, the student is likely to misjudge the time necessary to finish the remainder of the questions.

Test Grades Should be Prescriptive

A test grade should do more than provide for easy recording and reporting. The test grade should do more than give the pupil a rough idea of how they did relative to classmates. Teachers should make a deliberate effort to explain how questions were graded. An A- or D- at the top of the page or at the end of an essay adds very little, if anything, to a specific explanation of the quality or problems with a paper. We favor the use of numerical grades whenever possible because it is at least possible to see how the total was determined. As grades increase in their subjectivity they decrease in prescriptive quality. The teacher who is administering A's and D's with little regard for objectivity is insuring that the same pupils will receive similar grades the next time they are graded.

Tests Should be Returned Immediately

Nothing will undermine the importance of testing as a part of instruction quicker than not having exams returned immediately. The longer the exams remain ungraded or in the hands of the teacher the less the instructional value of the exam. The fact that papers or exams are not returned quickly may be related to a lack of teacher time for grading. We are convinced that this lack of time explains why so many tests are given on Friday. We favor a quick return of work coupled with a prescriptive grading system for maximum instructional effectiveness. Tardy or nonexistent feedback of test results has a devastating effect on pupil motivation. The student is left to conclude that the teacher is administering the tests as some form of busy work. This assumption commonly leads to an "If the teacher doesn't care, why should I care?" attitude. An attitude like this can only lead to poor test performance. Students will perceive the value of tests from the way they see the teacher manage the tests. If tests are important to you then they will be important to students. You can demonstrate that importance with a quick return time.

Tests Should be Reviewed for Bad Items

Occasionally you are going to include a confusing, poorly written or inappropriate question on a classroom test. You will know you have done this because students will raise questions during the test about the controversial question. The best advise we can give you is to have the students answer the question the best that they can at the time, but do an item analysis on the test before you assign grades.

A simple item analysis is a question by question count of incorrect responses. If everyone missed number 11, two things may have ocurred. First, the question may have been poorly written or confusing. Second, you may not have covered that particular point in class or, if you did, it was not taught as clearly as it could have been. If a question is confusing or inappropriate then drop it from the test before you compute a final grade. Grade the test as if the confusing question was not a part of the test. If everyone gets a question correct then maybe you did a good job on the content and followed that up by writing a good test question. An item analysis can be done very quickly with one other person's help. You might ask a student who has not been doing too well to help you during his or her study hall. If a bad question hurts a student's grade it has also hurt your performance as a teacher.

CONSTRUCTING INDIVIDUAL ITEM TYPES

Individual item construction is the heart of effective classroom testing. As the teacher, you want to determine if your students have learned what you believe you have taught them. A good test item, regardless of the specific type, has several characteristics. First, a test-wise student should not have an advantage over a less skilled test taker. Second, questions should minimize the possibility of guessing correct responses. Third, the vocabulary of the items should be familiar to the student. Do not rephrase questions in strange or unfamiliar vocabulary just to make them more difficult. Six common item types will be presented. An appropriate example of the item will be presented and the positive characteristics of each example will be discussed.

Matching Items

Matching questions commonly present two lists. Items in one list are called the premises and items in the other list are called the responses. Matching exercises can be used to measure the student's ability to discriminate between similar stimuli such as names, dates, places, etc. Good matching exercises have several characteristics. First, they only address one type of content. As you can see in Figure 1, the responses are similar. Dates, places, battles, etc. are not included in this particular question. This type of question tests the students' ability to discriminate between related concepts. If dates were included in the responses, then the premises would have to ask for dates. The student could eliminate date

31

responses and name premises, thus increasing the probability of correctly guessing an answer.

Figure 1

Matching Item Example Question

I. Matching (2 pts. each)
   Put the letter of the correct answer in the blank beside the correct phrase.

   _____ 1. A rebirth of classical   A. Humanism

   _____ 2. Soldiers of Milan   B. Renaissance

   _____ 3. View of life where   C. Decameron
            man is the center.
                                        D. Frescoes

   _____ 4. Paintings on wet
            plaster.   E. Bellum

Figure 1 includes several more important characteristics. The points per question are included, the directions are clear and concise, the student is required to write in the appropriate response letter thus avoiding complicated line drawing, there are no clues in the responses like titles, ranks or position, the names are all simple and there are more responses than premises. This discourages the process of elimination as a test taking strategy. The most common mistake made in the construction of matching exercises is mixing the content type of responses and premises.

True-False (Alternative Response) Items

True-false items are the most popular form of alternative response test item. Any forced choice item (ie. yes or no, fiction or nonfiction) is commonly classified as an alternative response item. Figure 2 provides a typical example of the true-false portion of a classroom test.

Figure 2

True-False Example Question

II. True-False (2 points each)
Circle T for true and F for false.

T F 1. The soldiers of Milan were called Condottieri.

T F 2. Parchment and bellum were two types of materials used for imprinting.

T F 3. Fuedalism stressed the importance of life on earth.

T F 4. "Queen of Adriatic" was a giant statue that was worshipped by the people of Italy.

T F 5. A dictatorship means that one man rules.

Figure 2 illustrates important considerations in constructing true-false items. List the test points involved. Provide simple directions. Have students circle the T or F. This eliminates T's that look like F's and F's that could be T's. The circle is very distinct and easy to score. The objective being tested should be important and should have been stressed during instruction. Trivia should be avoided as content for true-false items. Words like "always", "never," "sometimes", and "rarely" should be avoided. True-false items test knowledge of basic facts and are commonly placed in the first part of a classroom test.

The use of true-false items should be more restricted than we commonly see in practice. These items are deceptively easy to write, however, they only test lower levels of learning. The are susceptible to the guess. We strongly discourage the over use of this item type.

Multiple Choice Items

Multiple choice items test the student's ability to form associations as well as make subtle discriminations between content goals. Multiple choice items commonly follow matching or true-false items and preceed fill-in-the-blank, short answer, and essay items.

Figure 3

Multiple Choice Example Question

III. Multiple Choice (2 pts. each)
Write the correct letter in the blank provided

_____ 1.) The Renaissance began in
A) Germany
B) Italy
C) France
D) Spain

_____ 2.) The Black Death began in
A) 1352
B) 1329
C) 1348
D) 1368

Figure 3 presents the important characteristics of multiple choice items. Multiple choice items are composed of a stem (the question), the correct alternative (the right answer) and distractors (terms that are similar to the right answer but are not correct). Directions should be simple and point values should be included. The goal being tested should be important. The selections (correct response and distractors) should be homogeneous. Figure 3 selections are all countries and dates. If names were included in either of the selections, the probability of a correct guess would be increased. If the stem is an incomplete sentence the grammar of the stem or response may aid in answer selection, therefore avoid ending a stem with "a" or "an".

Fill-In-the-Blank

The Fill-in-the-Blank item tests the students' recall or specific terms or concepts within the context of a sentence or statement that appears as a test question. Fill-in-the-Blank items commonly preceed short answer items and follow multiple choice items. Figure 4 provides several examples of Fill-in-the-Blank questions.

Figure 4

Fill-in-the-Blank Example Questions

IV. Fill-in-the-Blank (2 pts. each)
   Complete the sentence by placing the correct term in the blank provided.

1. One of the problems created by the growth of old cities and the emergence of new cities was _____.
2. The reform group against industrial conditions was called _____.
3. Representation in the House of Commons and an extended right to vote were the results of the legislation known as _____.

When constructing Fill-in-the-Blank items it is important to remember several points. Limit the length of items. Do no lift items directly from sentences within the text. Test important concepts or goals. Do not let the size of your blank serve as a clue to the answer. Lastly, limit the number of blanks within each item to one or two at the most. The most frequent mistake with Fill-in-the-Blank items is that they are constructed with too many blanks. It is critically important to remember that test items should serve the process of evaluating student knowledge of key concepts or goals and not serve the lesser motive of test length.

Short Answer Items

Short answer items are attractive as test items because of their versatility. Short answer questions can be used to test the student's knowledge of processes, procedures, lists, concepts and steps. More importantly, they have application in every field of study. Figure 5 presents some examples of short answer items.

Figure 5

Short Answer Example Questions

V. Short Answer (2 pts. each)
    Answer as completely as possible.

    1. Define the term Amendment.

    2. List the first four presidents of the
       United States.

    3. List and explain the steps in wood
       refinishing.

Short answer items should be very specific in what they require for a correct response. The questions that are asked should require brief responses. If your questions is complex, the answer will be more difficult to assess objectively. Short answer items should not suggest longer essay type responses.

Essay Questions

Essay questions are the least understood, most poorly written and most subjectively graded of all the item types. Four considerations are essential to the construction of an effective essay question. First, what do you want to assess? Second, how restricted should the question be? Third, how restricted should the response be? Fourth, how are you going to evaluate the response?

The first consideration addresses the point made earlier in this section about asking any test question. Are you trying to evaluate something or just include a question because it seems natural? Essay questions are excellent test items to evaluate analysis, synthesis, evaluation or problem solving goals. What you want to evaluate should guide how you ask the question, how the student will respond and how you will evaluate the response. An essay question like, "Discuss World War II", is an invitation to student revolt. It is a totally unrestricted question with an infinite number of possible responses. The author of such a question deserves everything they get in the way of student criticism. How could anyone fairly grade such a question? A structured essay question features specific objectives, deliberate questioning and suggestons for specific response format. Figure 6 includes this type of question.

Figure 6

Essay Type Example Question

VI. Essay Question (7 pts.)
     Answer completely using the vocabulary of
     the chapter on motivation.

(1) Present seven theories of motivation.
Include the major theorists and an example of
each theory in practice.

The wording of the essay question in Figure 6 is
typical of a restricted essay item designed to
evaluate the knowledge of concepts as well as
test the ability to apply that knowledge. The
test item has deliberate objectives. It would be
hard to bluff an answer to such a question.

We favor the more structured format of
essay questions. We believe teachers should know
what they want to evaluate. When teachers want
specific information, a restricted essay question
is a natural method for acquiring that information because the item tests specific objectives.

Perhaps the most appealing part of a
restricted essay question is the opportunity for
fair, objective appraisal of the student's
response. A poorly graded essay question usually
follows from a poorly written essay question. An
appropriate answer will follow more naturally
from a well written essay item. We believe such
a model answer should guide evaluation and should
be made available to each student as a model for
future essay responses. The random assignment of
points or a casual letter grade does little to
help the student understand why he or she received
a specific grade on the essay question. Such
grading practices do little to help the student

improve the ability to respond to essay questions. The model answer tells the student that testing is part of instruction and not something independent of instruction.

If you are interested in just seeing what a student can do with an unstructured essay question, then ask one. You do not have to grade it, you could just look it over and make general comments or have a class discussion about a response you thought was particularly good. Stay away from trying to grade "What is your opinion?" type essay questions. We can think of no quicker way to discourage students from expressing their own opinions or to train them to express the rote opinions of others than to begin grading their opinions. If a student's opinion receives a low grade, they will stop expressing their opinion.

Suggested Readings

Hills, John. Measurement and Evaluation in the Classroom. 2nd Ed. Charles E. Merrill Publishing Company: Columbus Ohio, 1981. 14-53.

Sax, Gilbert. Principles of Educational and Phychological Measurement and Evaluation. Wadsworth Publishing Company, Belmont, California, 1980. 53-144.

Tenbrink, Terry D., Evaluation: A Practical Guide For Teachers. McGraw-Hill Book Company, New York: 1974. 337-406

Thorndike, R. L. and Hagen, E. P. Measurement and Evaluation in Psychology and Education. 4th Ed. John Wiley and Sons, New York: 1977. 198-272

CHAPTER 4

INSTRUCTION AND EVALUATION: A LEARNING APPROACH

"Every day is just like the day
before. We listen, take notes
and get threatened with the test
on Friday. The same kids get the
A's and the same kids get the low
grades. I get the F." James (high
school sophomore)

In this chapter we hope to present a realistic, practical approach to organizing an instructional unit that includes the effective use of student evaluation to improve pupil performance and successfully integrates evaluation with instruction. We encourage practicing teachers and prospective teachers to consider adopting our approach into the realities of your job assignment. We have included what we feel are critical elements of classroom instruction.

(1) Low inference instructional goal indentification.
(2) Instructional methods that facilitate recall.
(3) Test construction techniques that aid accurate evaluation.
(4) Evaluation procedures that enhance instruction.

We will provide actual examples of instructional goal lists, three equivalent forms of the same test with explanations for their use and a sequenced, day by day, instructional plan that incorporates the four elements of quality classroom instruction we have highlighted above.

LISTING LOW INFERENCE INSTRUCTIONAL GOALS

Appendix 1 is a list of 25 low inference instructional goals taken from a high school world history textbook chapter on social protest.

Notice that each goal identifies the specific concept, list, definition or principle to be learned. Once this list has been established, the teacher has several immediate uses for it.

1. A ready reference on what will be taught.

2. A document to share with parents, administrators or students.

3. A guide to instruction and test item construction.

Low inference goal statements can be developed from text guidelines, the teacher's individual judgement or from consulting outside references beyond the textbook. The important consideration is that test items can be more easily written from low inference goal statements than from more complex statements of instructional intent.

ITEM WRITING AND TEST ORGANIZATION

The objective of test item writing and test construction is to create equivalent forms of the same test. In order to accomplish this task, we suggest the following steps:

(1) Identify the instructional goal.
(2) Construct three separate items for each goal.
(3) Make each item a different item type.
(4) Construct three separate tests with each instructional goal appearing on each test in a different item format.

Figure 1, presents a visual example of the relationship between an instructional goal and three separate item types that test the instructional goal.

Figure 1

The Relationship Between Instructional Goals
and Test Item Types

Instructional Goal: Three Revolutions Related to
Social Movement

        1) Enlightenment
        2) French
        3) Industrial

Multiple Choice: Which of the following was
not a revolution related to
the social movement?

        1) Enlightenment
   *2) Communist
        3) French
        4) Industrial

True-False: The enlightenment was a
revolution that effected the
social movement. T F

Completion: List the three revolutions
that effected the social
protest movement.

        1) _____
        2) _____
        3) _____

Each of these item types would appear on separate
tests as illustrated in Appendix 2, 3 and 4.
Naturally, similar item types would be combined
on each test and the guidelines for test planning
and organization would be followed as suggested
in Chapter 3.

Perhaps the most dramatic difference in organizing an instructional unit around low inference instructional goals and three separate, equivalent forms of the same test is that the teacher can use the goal statements and tests to guide and direct instruction through the unit. Each of the tests could technically be used as a diagnostic instrument, although it is usually safe to assume that most students would have little advance knowledge of the subject matter. In practice, two forms of the test might be used as formative evaluations. The teacher could have students score the test in class. This would provide yet another opportunity for students to learn important unit goals. More realistically, you could administer a different form of the test at the end of the unit, to each section or period of the course. This might help overcome the inevitable sharing of answers that sometimes occurs between classes.

INSTRUCTIONAL METHODS THAT FACILITATE RECALL

We would like to suggest that each of the following activities has been shown, in various research reports and studies, to enhance memory, recall and test performance. Figure 2 presents the variables and an example of each variable operationalized in an instructional unit.

Figure 2

Instructional Strategies that Improve
Pupil Test Performance

---

1. Use of Advanced Organizers	- Telling students what they need to know.
2. Use of Mnemonic Devices	- Memory strategies that facilitate recall.
3. Distributed Practice	- Multiple opportunities to practice across time.
4. Formative Evaluations	- Opportunities to test what has been mastered.
5. Anxiety Reduction	- Nonthreatening practice

44

ORGANIZING THE INSTRUCTIONAL UNIT

The identification of low inference instructional goals and the construction of multiple, equivalent forms of the same test is only the first stage in delivering a quality instructional unit. The second stage is organizing the instruction and presentation of the unit within the context of a series of fifty-five minute class periods. We offer the following daily sequence as an alternative that permits application of instructional strategies that produce learning and testing procedures that improve instruction and pupil performance. Figure 3 presents a visual display of an instructional unit. An explanation and rationale for each days activities follows Figure 3.

Day One:

When students know precisely what they are expected to know, the probability of high performance is increased. The research literature is very clear on the topic of advanced organizers. We suggest providing students with a copy of the instructional goal list. They will know from the first day of the unit what is expected. Both you and the students will share the same frame of reference. Once the advanced organizer has been distributed you may begin direct instruction. You may choose to lecture, demonstrate or discuss, but the unit is under way.

Day Two:

A quick review of goals presented on day one provides a warm-up and distributed practice. More direct instruction may follow on the objectives listed next on the goal sheet. Your direct instruction can be as elaborate as you like. We suggest you provide time for peer teaching at the

45

Figure 3

Daily Plan for Instructional Unit

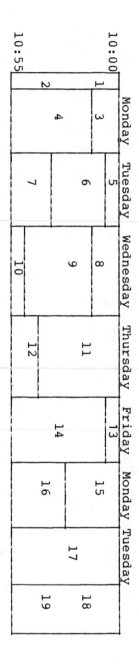

	Monday	Tuesday	Wednesday	Thursday	Friday	Monday	Tuesday
10:00	1 3	5 6	8 9	11	13 14	15	18
	2 4	7	10	12		16 17	19
10:55							

Pre-Instruction Activity
1. Low Inference Goals Identified and Listed
2. Equivalent Forms of Test Developed

Instructional Activity
3. Instructional Goals Distributed
4. Direct Instruction Goals 1-6
5. Review Goals 1-6
6. Direct Instruction 7-14
7. Peer Practice of Goals 1-14
8. Formative Evaluation 1-14
9. Student Grading 1-14
10. Reteach Goal # 12
11. Direct Instruction 15-21

12. Peer Practice and
    Rehearsal
13. Review 1-21
14. Direct Instruction 21-25
15. Peer Practice
16. Formative Evaluation 14-25
17. Summative Test

Post Instruction Activity
18. Test scoring and Item
    Analysis
19. Test Recording

conclusion of this day. Students can rehearse recall of basic facts and you are free to answer questions, encourage and motivate.

Day Three:

Since you have progressed through over half the unit goals, this might not be a bad time to see how much the students are remembering. You could administer one of the tests you developed or simply call out questions from the goal sheet and have students answer on a separate sheet of paper. The students could grade the test. You might have time to reteach a confusing goal or clarify a frequently missed question. At the conclusion of the third day of instruction your students have interacted with the first fourteen goals at least seven times.

Day Four:

Direct instruction continues on the next goals More peer teaching will provide opportunities to review previous goals as well as master more recent material. You are also free to monitor individual student progress and make suggestions on ways to memorize or problem solve.

Day Five:

A fairly lengthy review may be in order. You should begin to recognize student mastery of the first goals presented. The opportunities for rehearsal have been numerous. Direct instruction on the remaining objectives sets up a day of practice and review prior to the summative evaluation.

Day Six:

This is a good day to relax and review. A formative evaluation to diagnose goals that have not been mastered might improve performance on the summative test. You may wish to answer last minute questions or make suggestions for studying. You are in an excellent position to <u>help</u> them prepare for the major test to follow.

Day Seven:

Your students should be well prepared. Hopefully their anxiety is minimial and they are ready to show you what they know. Your test has been constructed since the beginning of the unit so you haven't been up all night trying to remember what you taught.

This chapter would not be complete without a mention of how grades are recorded, which grades are recorded and lastly how grades are assigned. The score on a pretest could be recorded. If you wish to grade according to individual progress you will have a grade to compare against. You will also be able to have some idea of the progress you are making instructionally. We recommend that scores on the formative evaluation also be recorded, but not figured in any average. These scores will tell you something about your own instructional effectiveness plus provide baseline data for evaluating whatever instructional style you used. We, of course, think summative scores must be recorded. If all has gone well the scores should be high. These are the scores you should use to compute six weeks grades, semester grades, and final grades.

This approach does not always have to be seven days in length. If you lecture two days instead of one, what difference does it make? What is important is that you follow the sequence and only use the summative grade to figure averages. If you were to do something like average the three grades together and call that a unit grade you would be defeating your purpose. You want the student to begin the next unit full of the motivation that has come from a recent excellent grade.

This instructional approach requires some unique behaviors from the teacher. You will have to make up three test items for each goal. you will have to be at least a week ahead of yourself in planning and test construction. You will still be able to deliver the great American lecture but you will have time to make it a good one. You will have to be willing to let students work with each other in class. You will have to be willing to let them score formative evalutions.

ELEMENTARY ACADEMIC EVALUATION: AN EXAMPLE

We offer the following example of a strategy for incorporating formative evaluations that are both objective and subjective into instructional units. We suggest, as we have above, that low inference goal identification is a requisite for effective planning at the elementary level. Once you have provided for direct instruction and pupil practice, a verbal review, in the form of a class meeting, can be an effective method for encouraging mastery.

Should you decide to develop formal test items to objectively assess performance, consider the following. Recognition type items (the answers appear in the test question) are excellent items for formative evaluations. Recall type items (students provide the answers) are excellent items for assessing the actual memorization of a concept, term, definition, etc. Formative tests that feature recognition items may enhance the student's confidence and reduce anxiety on the summative evaluation. At the elementary level, the student's belief that they can do well is as critical a consideration as their innate ability to master a task. Appropriate classroom test construction can assist that important confidence building.

49

Suggested Readings

Mayer, R. E. "Can Advanced Organizers Influence
    Meaningful Learning." in Review of Educational
    Research. Vol. 29, No. 2, Spring 1979.
    371-383.

Belleza, F. S. "Mnemonic Devices: Classification,
    Characteristics and Criteria." Review of
    Educational Research. Vol. 51, No.2, Summer
    1981. 247-275.

Brophy, J. "Teachers Praise: A Functional Analy-
    sis." in Review of Educational Research. Vol.
    51, No. 1, Spring 1981. 5-32.

APPENDIX 1

LOW INFERENCE INSTRUCTIONAL GOALS
(CHAPTER EXAMPLE)

---

1. Charles Dickens
   (1) wrote the novel, Hard Times.

2. The novel, Hard Times
   (1) protest against evils of industrialism.

3. Three Revolutions
   (1) Enlightenment
   (2) French
   (3) Industrial

4. Seven problems (Deadly Sins) caused by the Industrial Revolution.
   (1) unsanitary and dangerous factories
   (2) long working hours
   (3) child labor
   (4) exploitation of women
   (5) low wages
   (6) slums
   (7) recurring unemployment

5. Six problems created by the growth of old cities and the emergence of new cities.
   (1) unpaved streets
   (2) insufficient water supplies
   (3) poor lighting
   (4) tuberculosis and epidemics
   (5) poor living conditions
   (6) fire-danger in tenement districts

6. Leaders of the industrial revolution
   (1) favored laissez-faire capitalism

7. Two advocates of laissez-faire capitalism
   (1) Adam Smith
   (2) Thomas Malthus

8. Social Protest Movement
   (1) began in the 18th Century

9. Three principles set forth in the "Iron Law"
   (1) if population increases, then labor
       supply increases.
   (2) this increase causes competition for
       jobs, thus keeping wages from rising.
   (3) if labor supply declines and wages rise,
       then workers would produce more chidren
       and labor market would become glutted.

10. Two reasons that government was unable to
    improve conditions for factory workers.
    (1) it would only make conditions worse for
        workers.
    (2) government intervention would interfere
        with the law of supply and demand.

11. Tories
    (1) reform group against industrial condi-
        tions

12. Four achievements of the Tories.
    (1) labor unions were made lawful.
    (2) tariffs on imported grain was lowered.
    (3) harsh criminal code revised.
    (4) Roman Catholics and Nonconformists were
        permitted to hold office.

13. Reform Bill of 1832
    (1) gave representation in the House of
        Commons to the new industrial towns of
        the north.
    (2) extended the right to vote, thus grant-
        ing a share of political power to the
        new business class.

14. Three achievements of the "Reform Parliament"
    (1) abolished slavery in the British Empire
    (2) revised the poor laws.
    (3) liberalized municipal government.

15. Three acts that helped change factory conditions.
    (1) Act of 1833
    (2) Act of 1842
    (3) Ten Hours Act of 1847

16. Act of 1833
    (1) regulated employment of children in factories

17. Act of 1842
    (1) prohibited use of women, girls, and young boys in underground mines.

18. Ten Hours Act of 1847
    (1) established the principle of ten hours as normal working day.

19. Socialism
    (1) the ownership, management, and control of all means of production should be placed in the hands of the workers or the government.

20. The goal of the Utopian Socialists
    (1) to transform society into a harmonious community based upon the principles of cooperations and economic planning.

21. Most effective Utopian Socialist
    (1) Robert Owen

22. Karl Marx
    (1) introduced a new socialism called scientific socialism.

23. Two major works by Karl Marx.
    (1) Das Kapital
    (2) Communist Manifesto

24. Communist Manifesto
    (1) embodied principles of Marxian socialism
    (2) set forth a complete strategy for social revolution

25. Six basic beliefs of Marx
    (1) changes occur in history primarily
        because of economic factors.
    (2) the way goods are produced determines
        the character of society.
    (3) the group controlling the production of
        goods also controls society itself,
        therefore its laws, government, religion
        and culture.
    (4) the ruling group changes as the form of
        production changes.
    (5) all significant changes come about
        through class struggle.
    (6) labor theory of value - value of any
        product depends upon the amount of work
        necessary to produce it.

Name _____

TEST 1

I. MATCHING
   Directions: Place the letter from Column B
   in the blank in Column A. Items
   in Column B may be used only
   once or not at all. (5 points
   each).

Column A   Column B

___ 1. Charles Dickens   A. most effective Utopian
                             socialist

___ 2. Karl Marx   B. Hard Times

___ 3. Robert Owen   C. An Essay on the Prin-
                             ciples of Population

___ 4. Adam Smith   D. advocate of laissez-
                             faire capitalism

                          E. Das Kapital

                          F. important figure in
                             the development of
                             Utilitarianism

II. MULTIPLE CHOICE
    Directions: Place the letter of the correct
    answer for each statement on
    the line at the left. (2 points
    each)

___ 1. The novel Hard Times
       A. protested the evils of industrialism
       B. protested the start of the Industrial
          Revolution
       C. protested the principles of indus-
          trailism

55

_____ 2. The Social Protest Movement began in the
A. 17th Century
B. 18th Century
C. 19th Century

_____ 3. The Tories' achievements concerning
improved industrial conditions were
many. One of the achievements of the
Tories was
A. to have labor unions made lawful
B. to improve conditions in underground
mines
C. to control the law of supply and demand

_____ 4. One of the three acts that helped change
factory conditions was the
A. Act of 1852
B. Act of 1835
C. Act of 1842

_____ 5. Scientific socialism was a new type of
socialism introduced by
A. Adam Smith
B. Karl Marx
C. Robert Owen

III. SHORT ANSWER (4 points each)
Directions: Answer briefly using specific
terms in the unit.

1. List the three revolutions that led to a
new attitude toward the structure of
society.

2. List the three principles set forth in the
"Iron Law."

3. Explain the Act of 1847

4. Define socialism

5. List the two principles of the Communist
Manifesto.

56

IV. COMPLETION

Directions: Complete each sentence by writing in the correct answer (word or phrase) in the blank to the extreme left. (5 points each)

_____ 1. One of the problems created by the growth of old cities and the emergence of new cities was

_____.

_____ 2. The reform group against industrial conditions was called

_____.

_____ 3. Representation in the House of Commons and an extended right to vote were the results of the legislation known as _____.

_____ 4. The act that prohibited the use of women, girls, and young boys in underground mines was _____.

V. TRUE/FALSE

Directions: Circle true if the statement is true or false if the statement is false. (2 points each)

True   False   1. Leaders of the Industrial Revolutation favored government regulation of business.

True   False   2. One reason why government was unable to improve conditions for factory workers was that government intervention would interfere with the law of supply and demand.

True   False   3. The "Reform Parliament" achieved in making labor unions lawful.

57

True   False   4. The Act of 1833 prohibited the
                    use of women, girls and young
                    boys in underground mines.

True   False   5. The goal of the Utopian social-
                    istics was to transform society
                    into a harmonious community
                    based upon laissez-faire princi-
                    ples.

VI. ESSAY
     Directions: Limit the answer to the follow-
                 ing essay question to 100 words
                 or less. (10 points)

1.   List and explain four of the Seven Deadly
     Sins of the Industrial Revolution.

APPENDIX 3

Name _____

TEST 3

I. <u>COMPLETION</u>
Directions: Complete the sentence by writing in the correct answer (word or phrase) in the blank to the left. (3 points each)

_____ 1. The two advocates of laissez-faire capitalism were _____ and _____.

_____ 2. The social protest movement began in the _____ Century.

_____ 3. According to the Act of 1847, how many hours were considered a normal working day? _____

_____ 4. Labor unions were made lawful under the efforts of the reform group called the _____

II. <u>MULTIPLE CHOICE</u>
Directions: Place the letter of the correct answer for each statement on the line at the left. (3 points each)

_____ 1. The revolutions promoting social change were
a. French, Enlightenment, and Industrial
b. Industrial, Scientific, and French
c. French, Industrial and Literary

59

_____ 2. The prohibition of the use of
women, girls, and young boys in
underground mines was a result of
the
a. Act of 1833.
b. Act of 1842
c. Ten Hours Act of 1847.

_____ 3. An achievement of the Reform Parliament was
a. to liberalize municipal government.
b. to regulate employment of children in factories.
c. to lower tariffs on imported
grain.

_____ 4. Which of the following is a reason
government was unable to improve
conditions for factory workers?
a. the workers were on strike
b. the population was increasing
too fast
c. government intervention would
interfere with law of supply and
demand.

_____ 5. The Act of 1833 concerned what
group of people?
a. children
b. women
c. men

III. <u>TRUE-FALSE</u>
<u>Directions</u>: Circle true if the statement is
true and false if the statement
is false. (2 points each)

True   False   1. The most effective Utopian
Socialist was Thomas Malthus.

True   False   2. Charles Dickens wrote the novel,
<u>The Wealth of Nations.</u>

60

True   False   3. One of the principles of the
                  "Iron Law" is that if the popu-
                  lation increases, the wages
                  will increase.

True   False   4. The novel, Hard Times, was a
                  protest against the evils of
                  industrialism.

IV. MATCHING
    Directions: Place the letter of the item in
                column B that corresponds to the
                item in column A in the space
                provided. Items in column B can
                be used only once or not at all.
                (3 points each)

        Column A   Column B

___ 1. Utopian socialist   a. reform group against
                              industrial conditions

___ 2. socialism   b. favored by leaders
                              of the Industrial
                              Revolution

___ 3. Tories   c. protested against
                              the evils of indus-
                              trialism

___ 4. Laissez-faire   d. group in favor of
       capitalism   transforming society
                              through cooperation
                              and economic planning

                           e. ownership, management,
                              and control of all
                              means of production
                              should be placed in
                              hands of workers or
                              government

61

V. SHORT ANSWER   (7 points each)

1. List the seven problems caused by the Industrial Revolution (known as the Seven Deadly Sins).

   a._____

   b._____

   c._____

   d._____

   e._____

   f._____

   g_____

2. List the two accomplishments of the Reform Bill of 1832.

   a._____
     _____

   b._____
     _____

3. List the three acts that helped change factory conditions.

   a._____
   b._____
   c._____

VI. ESSAY
    Directions: Limit the answer to the following essay question to no more than 100 words. (10 points each)
1. Discuss the problems associated with the sudden growth of old cities and the emergence of new cities.

62

APPENDIX 4

Name _____

I. COMPLETION
   Directions: Complete each sentence with the
              correct word or phrase in the
              blank to the right of the sen-
              tence. (4 points each)

1. The author of the novel Hard Times is _____

2. The novel Hard Times was a protest against
   _____.

3. The statement "If population increases, labor
   supply increases is one of the principles of
   the _____.

4. The ownership, management and control of all
   means of production should be in the hands of
   the workers or government is the main idea of
   the form of government known as _____

5. Karl Marx's new socialism was called _____

II. TRUE-FALSE
    Directions: Circle true if the statement is
               true or false if the statement
               is false. (4 points each)

1. The French Revolution, the   True False
   Enlightenment, and the Indus-
   trial Revolution, all promoted
   economic change.

2. The problems caused by the   True False
   Industrial Revolution were
   known as the seven deadly sins.

3. Adam Smith and Thomas Malthus   True False
   were advocates of Laissez-Faire
   Capitalism.

63

4. The Social Protest Movement   True False
   began in the 17th Century.

5. The Reform Bill of 1852 gave   True False
   representation in the House
   of Commons to new industrial
   towns of the North.

III. SHORT ANSWER
    Direction: Provide a short answer for each
                of the following. (4 points each)

1. List four of the problems created by the
   growth of old cities and the emergence of
   new cities.

2. List the 4 achievements of the Tories.

3. List the 3 achievements of the Reform Parliament.

4. Discuss the goal of the Utopian Socialists.

5. List 3 of the basic principles of Marxian
   Socialism.

IV. MULTIPLE CHOICE
    Directions: Place the letter of the correct
                answer for each statement on the
                line at the left. (4 points each)

____ 1. Leaders of the Industrial Revolution
        favored
        A. Government regulation of business
        B. Socialism
        C. Laissez-Faire Capitalism

____ 2. The Tories were the reform group against
        A. Economic conditions
        B. Industrial conditions
        C. Social conditions

_____ 3. The most effective Utopian Socialist was
     A. Robert Owens
     B. Karl Marx
     C. Adam Smith

_____ 4. The major novel written by Karl Marx was
     A. The Wealth of Nations
     B. Das Kapital
     C. Communist Manifesto

_____ 5. The writing that embodied principles of
Marxian Socialism and set forth a complete strategy for social revolution was
called
     A. Communist Manifesto
     B. Das Kapital
     C. Scientific Socialism

V. ESSAY

    Limit answers to 100 words or less.(10 points)

1. List and explain the three acts that helped
to change factory conditions.

CHAPTER 5

FEELING AND COUNTING: THE ART AND SCIENCE OF EVALUATION IN ELEMENTARY SCHOOLS

"Yes, there is something better
than a test. Love is better than
a test." -Adrienne (4th grade)

The evaluation process is the most demanding activity required of the elementary school teacher. The decisions that will be made have enormous consequences for the students, teacher, and the program. These decisions affect the development of programs, the instruction within programs, and the evaluation of student academic and social progress. Evaluation decisions, requiring attention to three separate areas of influence, are never as simple as they first appear. At one level the teacher must evaluate the appropriateness of a specific program and it's instructional content. Is the program too difficult for the grade level? Perhaps it is too easy. Is it appropriate or inappropriate for continued academic success? The outside forces acting on evaluation decisions include the general community, district administrators, and specific parents. A second level involves the classroom. Does the classroom environment complement instructional goals? What curriculum materials are available within the class? Do the curriculum materials match the child's abilities? What are the teacher's abilities? A third level of influence is the pupil. Should this student be tested today? How has the student progressed? What weight should subjective considerations have in evaluation decisions?

In brief, the evaluation process in the elementary school is a complex process. The complexity of the process and the forces shaping it are the major causes of inadequate and inappropriate evaluation procedures. This segment of the text examines the different factors influencing the evaluation process and offers insights and suggestions that will permit you to develop evaluation techniques that are compatable with your personal philosophy, school district expectations, and your students' needs.

SCHOOL DISTRICT EMPHASIS

The well organized, successful school district usually has an established set of policies, goals, and priorities for the educational program. Districts select and develop curriculum materials based on identified goals and priorities. School districts then periodically evaluate student progress to determine programmatic strengths and weaknesses.

In the mid 1960's, school districts were generally satisfied with a general level of programmatic evaluation. However, accountability and back-to-basics movements began to force educators to examine specific student competencies. Student evaluation assumed additional importance as districts began to asses specific individual progress. Recently, more districts are requiring students to master basic skills and possess specific knowledge before advancing beyond a particular grade level. Other districts are at the stage of developing competency tests that eventually will determine whether or not a student can graduate. Increased pressures for teacher and student accountability are resulting in requirements for the development of more specific evaluation programs.

Norm-Reference Evaluation

General programmatic evaluations are referred to as norm-referenced testing procedures. Norm-referenced evaluation, in practice, refers to how well a specific child, classroom, or grade level performs in relation to the "average" child. Average is determined by the test developers and is based on test standardization. The test is administered to a large representative sample of children, the scores computed, and then the mean

68

(average) and score distribution are identified.
The child's and the group's score are then compared to the normative standards.

Standardized norm-referenced tests evaluate
general student abilities and general student
achievement levels. These measures do not indicate each student's strengths or weaknesses.
Because the tests are developed for large scale
evaluation and use, the developers do not tend to
include specific items that school districts
might emphasize in their particular curriculum
scope and sequence. Norm-referenced tests do not
measure student progress in relation to the
objectives and skills taught by the individual
teacher. Rather, they only measure general abilities based on items selected by the test devel-
oper. Standardized achievement and IQ tests may
indicate general areas of student strength and
weakness, but are not effective diagnostic
measures of specific growth and progress.

Norm-referenced evaluations may assist a
school district's programmatic evaluation. Evaluations of this type assist the district in identifying strengths and weaknesses within the program. Below are two examples of typical program
evaluations using norm-referenced tests.

A district recently found that its
children were scoring below the national
average in spelling. Concern for the
low performance led to a re-examination
of programmatic goals and an examination
of the spelling curriculum. The district
then decided to alter spelling policies
and goals, adopt a new textbook, and provide a series of inservice meetings for
teachers. At the end of the year tests
were administered to students to determine
the program's success.

Another school district was trying to
determine which math textbook series to

purchase for elementary arithmetic.
Two books were selected for test purposes and used in different classrooms. At the end of the year students took achievement tests. The
achievement results were used to
help determine which textbook series
the district adopted.

"When tests are used to compare individuals
with others, they provide norm-referenced inter-
pretations..." (Sax, 1980, p.22). Comparative
data obtained may be useful in evaluating programmatic effectiveness and general student abilities, but norm-referenced measures are limited
in that specific objectives and skills are not
generally evaluated.

Criterion Referenced Evaluation

"...when pupil progress is interpreted by
indicating what the individual is able to do
(e.g., a typing rate of forty words per minute,
or at least ten words spelled correctly per week,
or the student has read 12 pages in a specified
text), the interpretation is referred to as
criterion-referenced." (Sax, 1980, p. 22).

Criterion-referenced tests serve a different
evaluation function. Measurement of specific
student content and skill mastery is achieved
using criterion-referenced tests. Unit, grade
level or graduation objectives are specified and
criterion-referenced tests determine mastery levels relative to the specified outcomes. Teachers
using behavioral and instructional objectives
evaluate students progress in terms of the stated
objectives. For example, if an objective states
that the students will be able to list three
effects of pollution in their town, then the
evaluation would require students to list the
three effects. A student indicating three

acceptable responses will have met the criterion for that objective. As another example, graduation requirements might require that students balance a checkbook. Evaluation would require the student to actually balance a given checkbook. Students correctly balancing the checkbook have demonstrated mastery of the criterion identified in the objective. Criterion-referenced tests do not compare the child to others (a norreferenced comparison), they are designed to measure student mastery of specific objectives. A student that has demonstrated mastery has met the objective.

Individualized and self-paced educational programs frequently utilize criterion-referenced evaluation procedures. As illustrated in Figure 1, the process begins with the identification of program skills and objectives. Students are then pre-tested to determine their entry level and assigned objectives commensurate with their skill level. As they complete activities for each objective they are tested to determine whether or not the objective has been mastered. Mastery permits the child to continue the learning sequence while failure to master the objective results in an assignment of additional activities or instruction that will help the student master the objective. Criterion-referenced tests help the teacher individualize instruction because students' entering abilities are identified in relation to the sequence of objectives. The instructional sequence of pretest, instruction, and posttest allows students to begin instruction at the proper level and to progress at their own rate.

Figure 1

Pre-Post Test Model

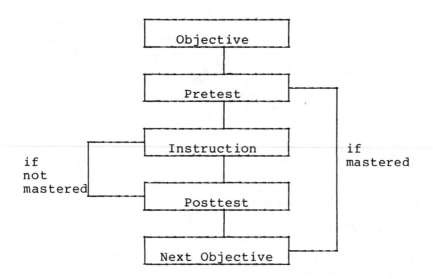

Criterion-referenced evaluations are not intended to compare students. An individual student's progress can only effectively be examined in terms of the progression through the instructional sequence. Criterion-based instructional models encourage the measurement of student progress along the instructional continuum. Because students have differing abilities, experiences, and achievement levels, comparisons with others can only be expressed by the number of skills mastered. Reports of progress within a criterion-referenced evaluation models tend to report the number of objectives mastered.

Criterion-referenced tests can also be useful for programmatic evaluations. Large numbers of students not meeting criteria for promotion or graduation would indicate that the obejctives are either not being taught or are inappropriate. In this sense, criterion measures may be useful for identifying programatic concerns. However, remediation may be difficult because evaluation may occur some time after the skills have been presented. Basic skill acquisition should be constantly monitored on a criterion-referenced basis - a sole reliance on results of promotion tests will not provide the immediate feedback necessary in the daily instructional process.

There apperas to be an increasing emphasis by school districts and the public to return to a basic, competency-based elementary education. An emphasis on academic basics and competency-based education requires students to acquire certain specified skills, knowledge, and behaviors. A school district concerned with competency-based education is more likely to utilize criterion-referenced evaluation models.

"Criterion-referenced measurement is an attempt to interpret test results in terms of clearly defined learning outcomes which serve as the criteria (or referents) for firming judgements." (Ten Brink, 1974, p. 74). Mastery of specific skills and progression through a sequential program are facilitated by criterion-referenced measures. The pre-post test model is an effective method.

Summary

School districts evaluate student progress for a number of reasons. Program improvement, response to public demands for accountability and facilitating skill mastery are among the important reasons school districts require student evaluation. Norm-referenced and criterion-referenced procedures were discussed as each contributed to an overall evaluation program.

From a job security standpoint, teachers must acknowledge the importance of following school district guidelines. Failure to comply adequately could result in a low teacher evaluation.

THE CLASSROOM

In addition to district mandates, teachers are confronted with a room full of active, individual students. Within the classroom context, teachers experience two additional evaluation considerations - at certain times students need to be evaluated according to their own individual abilities and in other situations evaluation by comparison is required. This section presents the situational appropriateness of individual and group comparisons.

Evaluations Based on The Individual

Each child begins life with a repertoire of behaviors similar to other children, but as the child develops, individual variations in acquired skills, knowledge and behaviors become apparent. There are significant differences in the quality and quantity of each child's knowledge and development. While there may be many normative similarities, no two children are at exactly the same level of development as individual growth patterns and abilities naturally vary from child to child. Instructional content, methods and evaluation must be designed to meet each child's individual educational needs. Evaluation techniques must ensure that each child's progress is accurately assessed and reported.

Successful kindergarten and sixth grade teachers are equally well aware of differences in individual needs and abilities. While many students may be ready for certain instruction, other students in the classroom may not have acquired the prerequisite abilities and will not benefit from the advanced instruction. An example encountered by the kindergarten teacher might

74

involve a decision to move a student on to a pre-primer level of reading instruction or to continue to help the student develop perceptual and time-on-task abilities. The sixth grade teacher might need to decide whether to continue multiplication instruction or move on to division instruction. Certain students will be ready for advancement in both instances while others may not be ready until much later.

The teacher must decide whether or not a student learned the skills necessary for advancement. The decision to advance should not be made on the basis of what is expected of the normal student at that age or grade, rather, the decision should be based on the student's readiness to proceed. Instruction designed for the entire group may prevent the slow or the gifted student from proceeding at a pace commensurate with individual needs and abilities. The slow student would become frustrated by working beyond his or her capabilities while the faster student might become bored and direct attention elsewhere.

Decisions pertaining to student placement and advancement are dictated by the curriculum sequence as well as by the needs and abilities of each individual student. Learning in subject areas such as reading and math must be based on the growth and development of each student. Differences in student abilities require teachers to evaluate each student as an individual. Optimum gains in achievement can only be realized when teachers consider each student's unique needs and differences.

Evaluation Based on Comparison

While individual evaluation is important, it follows from initial comparisons of other students. Group comparisons facilitate individual evaluations because comparisons help teachers identify the range of possible and probable classroom behaviors. For example, an inexperienced teacher might be concerned with one student's inability to begin work. A comparison with the work habits of others may indicate that the student's behavior is inappropriate. However, in many instances, the student in this example may exhibit the inappropriate behavior in limited situations. A closer examination may reveal that the student has trouble getting started when seated in a certain area of the room such as next to the science display. The teacher can make several conclusions. One, the student should not be seated near the science display other than during science. Secondly, the student likes science and is more interested in that particular display than other work. Aspects of the student's behavior are inferred from the situation as well as from the way other students behave in similar settings.

While a comparative approach is an outgrowth of the early twentieth century testing movement, a need for this type of evaluation remains necessary and purposeful. Not all aspects of the student's behavior are measureable in terms of subject matter learned or respective position along an achievement continuum. For example, teachers are required to report to parents and, while the parents want to know how well their child is doing according to his or her own ability, they also want to know how the child is progressing in relation to other students. The new, inexperienced teacher will need to make both child-to-child and child-to-group comparisons as he or she attempts to evaluate students. Additionally, students learn and are curious about their own relative class standing early in the elementary school. For these and a number of other reasons, teachers need to learn how to evaluate students on a comparative basis.

A teacher that only evaluates students in regard to individual progress could easily overlook the special needs of slow or fast students. Gifted students and students with learning disabilities may go unrecognized without adequate comparisons. Teachers need to be aware of the students' relative class standing and be ready to provide additional emotional support for those at both ends of the educational continuum. Furthermore, an awareness of the relative standing of students within the classroom will enable the teacher to better organize the room. Room organization and student grouping will enable a teacher to provide for student needs in a more efficient manner.

Many topics considered important in the elementary school, such as developing positive self-concepts and social interaction skills, are difficult to test or measure. Areas in the affective realm may be more effectively evaluated through observation and comparison with other students. Work habits, social skill development, motivation, coordination, interests, thinking level, imagination, creativity and learning style are often evaluated in terms of other students' actions and abilities. Subjective evaluations, based on comparisons with the work and behavior of other students, are necessary and inevitable because the teacher has expectations for the entire group.

Writing instruction serves as an example of a field in which subjective, comparative evaluation may be useful. During the past decade the emphasis on writing instruction has shifted from creative writing and expression of one's ideas to an emphasis on writing skills and mechanics. The elementary teacher can encourage writing mechanics and still subjectively evaluate creative writing projects. The teacher can compare student work as a means of identifying the more creative students while using objective criteria for monitoring individual skill development. The skills can be measured and plotted along a skill continuum, but the creative aspects of writing are too difficult to measure objectively and impossible to pinpoint in a developmental sequence. As this example suggests, some aspects of schooling cannot be objectively measured: a subjective, comparative assessment is necessary.

Comparative evaluations can help the teachers identify student behaviors that significantly differ from the norm. This type of evaluation is also useful to new teachers as they learn about the range of behaviors within a classroom. Subjective inferences can be made based on comparing an individual with his or her peer group. Teachers can then make certain judgements from comparative information.

A teacher must be a well trained observer to make appropriate comparisons and experience will help. The teacher's professional judgement is crucial to the artistic, subjective evaluation process.

Summary

Teachers make numerous decisions daily. These decisions are made within a dynamic, sometimes hectic environment called a classroom. Decisions about skills, behavior, attitudes and feelings must be made as teachers implement instructional strategies. Decisions such as what to teach and how to teach require teachers to examine individual needs and abilities as well as group characteristics. Therefore, teachers must analyze the classroom environment from an individual and group perspective.

TEACHER EMPAHSIS

Two domains of intellectual functioning are involved in the educational process: the cognitive, content domain and the affective, attitudinal domain. (Ellis, 1977) Because the elementary school curriculum focuses on sequential content, evaluation frequently focuses on content mastery. Experienced teachers, however, realize the need to develop positive attitudes toward school, learning and the subject matter. These

78

positive attitudes enhance a student's ability to master subject matter and facilitate the development of a positive self-concept, self-discipline, and appropriate social interaction skills.

Many cognitive forms of learning can be assessed objectively. That is, students can be tested to determine the knowledge and skills acquired. Affective goals and objectives cannot be measured as easily and may therefore be evaluated using subjective means. This portion of the chapter discusses objective and subjective evaluation techniques.

Objective Assessment

Effective planning requires teachers to identify specific instructional objectives, provide appropriate instructional activities, and evaluate student mastery of the specified objectives. This is essentially a criterion-referenced process because student progress is judged by a predetermined set of criteria. Student mastery is objectively measured - the student has either mastered or not mastered each objective.

Objective, criterion-referenced assessment need not be formal. Both formal and informal objective evaluations are useful in classrooms. Five objective techniques will be discussed in this section. The five methods - direct observation, grading daily papers, teacher made tests, published tests, and district level competency tests - range from informal to formal.

Perhaps one of the best methods for detecting learning problems is exemplified by the teacher who actively observes the students as they work, not from the teacher's desk, but by moving around the room looking as students are working. The teacher can ensure that students have begun work, are working on the correct assignment, and are not making errors. Students frequently misinterpret the teacher's directions and explanations. By moving about the room the teacher can determine whether or not the students have understood the instructions and whether or not they understand the concept. Children making errors can be counseled immediately and corrective measures taken. Additionally, by maintaining a closer proximity to the students the teacher can reduce the probability of disruptive behavior occurring.

An example of teacher movement illustrates the importance of this evaluation procedure. A third grade teacher had just presented instruction in multiplication. The students had worked several problems using counters and were ready to do a practice assignment. The teacher assigned the work, wrote the assignment on the board, and then began moving about the room. She first went by Robbie. Robbie always had trouble getting started and often had his book opened to the wrong page. After re-directing Robbie's efforts she moved to an area near Amy and Ann. Amy and Ann worked well together, but usually visited a little too much. The teacher's presence was enough to encourage the two girls to work quietly. With the entire group busily at work, the teacher then moved about the room watching students manipulate the counters as they solved the assigned problems. She happened to observe Jeff grouping counters the wrong way as he tried to discover the solution for 6 x 7 - he had seven groups with seven counters in each group. Jeff was asked to explain the counter arrangement which resulted in his discovering his own mistake. The teacher then watched as Jeff correctly solved the next problem.

As the teacher moved about the room she directed students toward the appropriate task and reduced discipline problems. From an evaluation perspective the teacher had corrected and

80

redirected students making errors before students had an opportunity to practice their mistakes.

Elementary teachers tend to spend a significant portion of their after school time correcting papers. This is an effective evaluation process because it allows the teacher to check student progress and plan future instruction based on student performance. For example, one teacher was teaching renaming addition to the ten's place. As she graded student practice papers she discovered that several students were carrying the renamed ten to the hundreds place. She adjusted the next day's instructional plans to correct the problem. This example illustrates how one teacher used the process of correcting daily work to modify instruction within an instructional sequence.

Teachers often need a slightly more formal method to determine the effectiveness of their instruction and the extent to which students master a skill. By constructing their own tests, teachers can quickly assess student learning. Teacher-made tests need not be lengthy. A teacher presenting a unit on mapping skills might ask children to construct maps following certain criteria. The teachers may also require students to locate items, such as those contained on a map key, as a means of determining student learning. A student that can identify and locate the symbol for an airport may have demonstrated map key mastery. A teacher that has taught the meaning of a certain prefix might simply ask students to identify or state another word in which the same prefix has the same meaning. Teacher constructed measures can be very brief and still remain useful. The main strength lies in the fact that the teacher is evaluating objectives and instruction he or she has determined necessary for particular students.

Periodic objective evaluations are often available from publishers of adopted textbook series. Usually textbook objectives are organized within a well defined scope and sequence and the tests accompanying the text book series evaluate student progress within the sequence. An additional advantage of using published tests is that teachers have an opportunity to examine the effectiveness of their ability to implement the materials relative to student needs.

The Scott, Foresman Math Series exemplifies an objective assessment procedure distributed for use with a textbook series. Instructional objectives and learning outcomes are identified and sequenced. The sequence is then divided into a series of units and each unit includes test items for the unit objectives. The test items can be used as a pretest. Students mastering the pretest can proceed to the next unit and those not mastering the objectives can be provided appropriate learning activities followed by a posttest included with the series. The teacher has observed students as they participate in the instructional activities, checked their daily work, evaluated students according to his or her own criteria, and administered the end-of-unit test when the students are ready.

The final objective evaluation technique involves the administration of district or state competency tests. As discussed earlier, this includes those examinations required for promotion or graduation. These measures have not been widely used in the past, but districts and states are beginning to develop competency-based examinations to determine whether or not students meet criteria deemed necessary at certain grade levels. Questions such as, "Should a student that can't figure simple interest be allowed to graduate from high school?" exemplify the concerns addressed by district and state competency examinations. Before a student receives a diploma certain minimum competencies must be demonstrated.

Generally any evaluation, whether formal or informal, can be considered objective if items evaluate student learning of specified objectives. The usefulness of objective evaluation can be both immediate, as in the case of direct teacher observation, or a distant check point, as in the case of district/state competency tests.

Subjective Assessment

The affective nature of student evaluation is also important. A student's attitude toward school, education, the teacher, and other children are important to continued academic growth. The nature of elementary education requires teachers to enhance appropriate attitudes as they interact with students. Evaluating affective, attitudinal characteristics is difficult. While trained psychologists have tests available, there are few useful standardized tests available for the classroom teacher's daily use. Evaluating affective characteristics requires teachers to use subjective methods.

Attitudinal goals and objectives are general and not easily measured. Social skills, for example, are important in any educational setting. Evaluating social skills cannot easily be done with a paper and pencil test. Such concepts as cooperation, group participation, and respecting others must be observed and inferred rather than objectively measured. The students' personal development is another area requiring emphasis that can not be easily measured. There are no measurement instruments for topics such as sense of humor, confidence, and blame acceptance. Evaluating topics such as these requires a teacher to examine the characteristics within the context of the students' environment, not according to a curricular scope and sequence.

Every teacher has one student that is particularly difficult to figure out. Arnold was such student. He was a nice boy, but did not like to do required work, had difficulty interacting with others, had frequent temper tantrums, and made offensive verbal utterances. Arnold was capable, but spent more time getting into compromising situations than necessary for a person his age.

It would have been very easy to ignore Arnold's problems, but one teacher decided that Arnold was not lost. Because no objective measures were available, the teacher was not sure where to begin. So, before beginning to attempt treatment, she collected information about the errant lad. She first used unobtrusive observation techniques that allowed her to watch Arnold interact within the school environment. That is, she observed his interactions with other students in the classroom and during recess. The teacher also watched the way Arnold behaved as he worked on individual assignments and within small group contexts. As the teacher observed Arnold, she recorded her observations. These anecdotal records proved helpful as she categorized observed behaviors and determined an appropriate plan of attack. Finally, the teacher administered a sociogram that helped her determine who Arnold liked and who liked Arnold. With this information the teacher began to plan a strategy. Before implementing the strategy, however, the teacher met with Arnold to determine his concerns and his reaction to portions of her strategy.

Arnold did not change over night, but gradual changes occurred. As certain actions worked they were reapplied and as other ideas failed, they were modified. Gradually, however, the teacher began to alter Arnold's behavior and by the end of the year Arnold was almost normal.

Professional judgement is necessary as teachers subjectively evaluate students. Art critics are usually well trained and have an excellent understanding of artistic production. They also have an artistic nature that enables them to go beyond the skills employed by an artist. Art critics examine the artist's skills as well as the composition's subjective, aesthetic nature. Teachers, much like art critics, need to look beyond objective skill analysis and subjectively examine the students' affective nature.

Subjective analysis can also help teachers plan instruction. While education is concerned with increasing the knowledge and skill base, certain instructional procedures might inhibit a student's attitude toward the topic. A lesson could conceivably increase learning while antagonizing the student toward that subject. Examples include the teacher that may assign additional work as punishment. The result may be a possible increase in mastery with a corresponding decrease in attitude toward the topic. Teachers may also deem content mastery so important that they fail to use appropriate motivational techniques as they present instruction - work becomes a drudgery in the absence of student motivation. Additionally, teachers have been known, on occasion, to require student reports even when they know that several students are extremely shy and bashful. Forcing shy and bashful students to report to the entire group may alienate them towards further efforts on their own. Teachers can and need to be task oriented, but they also need to temper their expectations and instructional methods to the needs, interests and personalities of students. Evaluating student enthusiasm may indicate that different methods are necessary to ensure that the objectives will be mastered while maintaining enthusiasm toward the subject. Students want to learn, and learning should be exciting. Attitudinal evaluation can provide useful feedback and result in instruction that increases student learning and attitudes.

Summary

Elementary-age students are undergoing tremendous physical, intellectual, personal and

85

social changes. Young children are leaving home, often for the first time, and are being forced to compete with others for materials and adult attention. While many children may be very bright, capable students, they might withdraw until they become comfortable within the new setting. With a greater number of divorces and single parent families, teachers are encountering a growing number of students coming from less than acceptable home situations. These students are preoccupied with external events and not able to concentrate effectively on their school work. Consider the third grade student who reported that he as kept awake well after midnight by a parental disturbance. This student was in no position to learn effectively nor to be tested the following day. The teacher needs to know, understand, and have the ability to assess individual progress in the content areas as related to the scope and sequence of the curriculum. But the teacher also needs to be a skilled observer of human interaction and be aware of the subjective nature of each student he or she works with. Simply stated: the elementary teacher must develop both the art and the science of evaluation. The art of evaluation is subjective in nature and based on the teacher's understanding of the comparative nature of what is normal and abnormal. The science of evaluation objectively measures student progress skills, knowledge, and behaviors acquired. Both are necessary and, in a sense, compliment each other as the teacher evaluates "the whole child."

CONCLUSION

    Evaluation should not be viewed as a necessary evil. While the public, school districts and parents place enormous demands on students, teachers need to act in the best interests of the students and society. The teacher's task is to ensure that evaluation procedures are used correctly and humanely. Evaluation should be seen as a method of obtaining instructional feedback at the district and classroom level. The dilemma is not one of deciding which, if any, evaluation format is the best. Rather, the teacher's task is to determine which evaluation format is appropriate in specific instructional situations. The teacher, as a professional, must be an artist and a scientist while evaluating students and their work. Evaluation is a process requiring the best in artistic and scientific interpretation. The teacher's most responsible and challenging moment is when asked to respond to a student's question, "How's my work?". The response is not just another moment in the life of a student.

References and Selected Readings

Ebel, Robert L. "Educational Tests; Valid? Biased? Useful?" Phi Delta Kappan 54: 85 October 1975.

Ellis, Arthur K. Teaching and Learning Elementary Social Studies. Boston: Allyn and Bacon, Inc., 1977.

Glasser, William Schools Without Failure. New York: Harper and Row, 1969.

Houston, W. Robert and Robert B. Howsome (eds.) Competency-Based Teacher Education. Chicago: Science Research Associates, Inc., 1972.

Sax, Gibert Principles of Psychological Measure-Ment and Evaluation, Second Ediction. Belmont, California: Wadsworth Publishing Company, 1980.

Ten Brink, Terry D. Evaluation: A Practical Guide for Beginners. New York: McGraw-Hill Book Company, 1974.

CHAPTER 6

THE WHOLE CHILD: EVALUATION CONSIDERATIONS

"They (teachers) could get
together with you privately
and ask you the kinds of
questions a test would have."
-Sonya (Grade 5)

This chapter examines the relationships
between educational goals, pupil evaluation, and
two evaluation philosophies. Educational goals
appropriate for the elementary school can be sub-
divided under four headings: intellectual, personal, social and health/physical. Subjective
and objective aspects of pupil evaluation will be
discussed in this chapter as they apply to the
goals. That is, evaluation emphasis will depend
on the nature of each goal. Finally, this
chapter discusses two current educational philosophies. An examination of the two philosophies
(behavioristic and phenomenological) will allow
teachers to examine how each philosophy is operationalized in student evalution. An examination
of these three topics will provide an understanding of how educational instruction and evaluation
affects the whole child.

ELEMENTARY GOALS

Elementary school goals can be grouped into
four general categories. The four categories,
illustrated in Figure 1, are: intellectual,
social, personal, and health/physical. Each goal
provides the outline for overall emphasis and is
translated into daily instructional objectives.
However, because several goals are long range,
they can not be specifically stated for short-
term lessons. Some goals can be easily measured
and others not easily measured.

Figure 1

Categories and Examples of
Elementary School Goals

Intellectual Goals	Personal Goals	Social Goals	Health/Physical Goals
Language Skills	Self-Concept	Appreciation of Arts and Culture	Development of Five Senses
Creative Thinking	Self-Discipline	Citizenship	Muscle Skills and Coordination
Problem Solving	Motivation	Cooperation With Adults	Health and Safety Habits
Academic Skills	Enjoy School and Learning	Cooperation with Children	Mental Health

Intellectual Goals

Intellectual goals include academic skills
such as the 3-R's and language skills because they
are designed to foster basic skill acquisition.
Creative thinking and problem solving are also
included in the intellectual category because they
require the student to process facts and apply
skills. Creative thinking and problem solving
are cognitive (intellectual) in nature and the
mental functioning required to process and apply
information proceeds from levels of lesser

90

complexity to levels of greater complexity. Furthermore, acquisition of knowledge is quantitative while processing information is qualitative, and intellectual development requires both.

An example of qualitative and quantitative intellectual change is seen in a child's early concept of number. A young child may first learn to count by rote, then quantities are identified by the child (such as two trucks or three dolls). Qualitative changes in the child's mental abilities are demonstrated in Piaget's conservation of number task (See Figure 2). Although preschool children may know how to count and identify groups of objects by number, they cannot process the qualitative changes that occur in the conservation of number problems. The preschool child will identify lengthened rows of pennies as having more. It is not until certain alterations in the child's ability to mentally apply and integrate information that the child will recognize the lengthened row as having the same number.

Figure 2

Conservation of Number

A.   0 0 0 0 0
      0 0 0 0 0

First ask the child to compare two equally spaced rows of pennies. The child should indicate that both rows have the "same" amount.

B.   0 0 0 0 0
      0 0 0 0 0

Next lengthen one row and ask the child which row has a greater number. Younger children do not have the qualitative abilities to analyze and understand the problem.

Personal Goals

Personal development is an important aspect of education. Such topics as self-concept, self-discipline, motivation, and enjoyment of school and learning are included in the elementary school curriculum. Self-assured students have mastered basic psychological states that allow them to pursue more distant needs. Such statements as, "Success leads to success" reflect the importance of feeling good about one's self. A student that feels good will be more willing to experiment and try new learning activities. Students with weak self-images are less likely to take chances in new situations.

Most teachers agree that there is a close relationship between personal goals and intellectual goals. For example Bill was a student who had a poor self-concept and was weak academically. He engaged in withdrawal and avoidance behaviors because he wanted to avoid further academic and personal failure. Bill was fortunate to have a certain student teacher work with him. Bill and the student teacher worked together on specific academic skills. The student teacher also bolstered Bill's ego as she accepted him as an individual. As Bill gained confidence in himself and a sense of self-worth, his academic performance improved.

Social Goals

Social goals are also important. Piaget (1950) stated that social interaction is one prerequisite to intellectual development. Children must learn to work and cooperate with others in order to become socialized. Eric Erikson (1967) stated that one of the conflicts elementary-aged students must resolve is that of industry versus inferiority. During this stage, students must learn the skills and conventions of their culture. Our culture includes social interaction skills and academic skills as necessary tools for success. Inability to learn appropriate social and academic

skills will lead to feelings of inferiority and
inhibit the development of a positive personal
identity.

Citizenship encompasses many of our society's
rules for interacting with one another. Citizenship skills, in a sense, help students identify
their place within society and methods by which
they can contribute to that society.

Aesthetic appreciation (appreciating the arts
and culture) allows students to learn more about
human potentialities. Pride as a group member can
be derived from aesthetic experiences. The arts
and cultural goals will also serve as vehicles for
applying cognitive abilities in novel and creative
ways. While citizenship sets parameters for
behavior, aesthetic experiences free the affective,
creative needs within the student.

Health/Physical Goals

Health/physical goals must not be overlooked.
Perceptual and motor development allow the individual to perceive and act on stimuli in the
environment. Perception and cognition develop
together as the child's mental abilities expand.
Motoric development helps the individual coordinate
actions. Students with perceptual and motor abilities usually progress less than satisfactorily in
school.

Many students with learning disabilities are
termed disabled because their perception and perceptual processing abilities have not matured sufficiently to allow them to master certain tasks.
Classic examples are illustrated by students unable
to acquire necessary reading and writing skills
because of reversals. Letters such as "b" and "d"
are often reversed as are words such as "was" and
"saw". Without the ability to process letters and
words correctly, the brain receives jumbled mes-
sages which do not make sense.

Another example of physiological weakness involves the inability to retain information on a short-term basis. Short-term memory is necessay for reading as students must retain the first part of a word or message as they attempt to decode the following portions. Short-term audio and visual memory, if not sufficiently developed, will limit the ability to learn because children can not remember information long enough to process it adequately.

Muscle skills and coordination also facilitate learning, self-concept, and social interaction. Hand-eye coordination is necessary for school subjects such as writing, physical education, and art. A student with poor coordination may suffer academically and socially. Other students may perceive the individual as awkward and therefore avoid such a child. This, in turn, could result in a lower self-esteem.

Martha was a fifth grade student who had gone several years with poor eyesight and an over-protective mother. Martha's visual problems were not detected until she entered school, at which time she was referred to an optometrist for glasses. Upon entering school, her hand-eye coordination was very weak and her muscle skills were underdeveloped because her mother placed limitations on exploratory behavior. As a result of uncorrected poor vision and inability to interact with environmental stiumli, Martha entered school well behind the other children. Martha was weak academically and socially.

Health and safety habits and the ability to cope are also appropriate for the elementary school. Elementary students are not knowledgeable nor sophisticated enough to know all the hazards in the world. Health, safety and coping skills can help prepare them for more independence.

Educational goals are important and interdependent. Students must not only learn the academic

94

skills necessary for adult life, they must learn how to apply that information in personal and social settings. Academic goals are important, but not at the expense of developing the whole child.

Summary

Each goal does not warrant the same amount of emphasis throughout the elementary grades. Parents and teachers recognize and tend to stress personal and social adjustment early in the elementary school experience while academic goals receive greater emphasis as the student matures. The kindergarten teacher must attend to school adjustment before considering academic performance. Most intermediate level students have adjusted to the personal, social, and academic demands and can direct more attention and energy toward academic goals. A fifth or sixth grade teacher does not need to spend as much time helping students learn to use school restrooms properly. Conversely, primary students do not have the attention span to work for long periods at one single task. The focus and emphasis placed on elementary goals changes as the student moves from one grade to the next.

The primary task of elementary education is to develop the "whole child". The range and number of goals underscore this purpose. The "whole child" is served as teachers provide cognitive and affective learning experiences. Intellectual functioning, (information acquisition and processing) helps the student develop competencies for later life and learning. Learning to read and compute are not ends in themselves. Reading and math skills allow the individual to acquire and use information for problem solving later in school and life. Affective functioning (developing positive attitudes) and interaction with others, help the individual solve problems and interact with others in appropriate ways. Attitudes are important in problem solving situations as personal feelings and attitudes are involved (Kaltsounis, 1979).

95

Evaluating the "whole child" requires teachers to consider the cognitive and affective nature of school goals. Student progress in both areas must be objectively and subjectively analyzed as teachers examine total growth and development. A quick glance at any elementary school report card will illustrate the emphasis placed on cognitive and affective goals.

OBJECTIVITY AND SUBJECTIVITY: A DELICATE BALANCE

A teacher can emphasize skill acquisition at the expense of the student's attitude toward school and learning. A student might master the subject content, but the subject itself could conceivably become distasteful. Thus, the likelihood of the student continuing to enjoy and pursue the topic would diminish and future encounters with that content area would be avoided.

Teachers must balance their instructional emphasis. Each goal area should receive appropriate emphasis from both cognitive and affective perspectives. The objective and subjective components of each goal are too important to be overlooked. Failure to balance the objective and subjective components inherent in elementary school goals may result in a critical inbalance. A teacher could have students that like school, yet have not learned. Conversely, students could learn a sufficient amount of information, but not like school and learning. The remainder of this section briefly discusses the objective and subjective nature of elementary school goals.

Intellectual Goals

Intellectual goals, by their very nature, are the easiest to evaluate. Reading, writing, math, language arts, science, and social studies goals are generally organized around well defined scope and sequence curricula. Each discipline progresses from relatively simplistic readiness levels to progressively more sophisticated levels. The student moves from level to level according to individual, small group or large group promotion. The objective and subjective emphasis placed on intellectual goals is visible in teacher selected instructional methods.

A teacher wishing to emphasize the objective dimension of a goal would typically elect to use teacher-directed instructional techniques. The teacher would first determine the specific skill and information and the skill would be directly taught. This interaction is teacher designed, teacher controlled and teacher evaluated. Students are passive participants in the learning process as the teacher's primary concern is to ensure retention and recall of content.

The pretest-instruct-posttest method exemplifies an objective approach. At the kindergarten level a teacher might determine that the long sound of the vowel "a" needs to be taught. The teacher would pretest students to identify their level of proficiency. Students not meeting the criteria level would then receive instruction and practice to strengthen that skill. At the end of the instructional sequence the teacher would assess skill acquisition through a posttest.

A sixth grade teacher might be interested in the students' social studies knowledge about a geographic area. Again, a pretest would be administered, followed by instruction and practice. The end of the instructional sequence would include a posttest.

Teachers choosing to utilize a subjective approach would rely on student-centered instructional methods. The teacher would consider the students' intellectual needs, motivation and learning interests. According to this approach, students are viewed as being competent learners and capable of self-directed learning. Programs based on a subjective approach provide appropriate learning activities that parallel content objectives.

97

Pupil competence is encouraged through activities that direct the student toward appropriate terminal goals. Interaction with materials, other students, and the teacher are essential. The teacher is a guide while the student's internal desire to master his or her own world provides the motivation for academic learning.

Experienced teachers know that the best opportunity for learning occurs when the students are motivated. Students often show an interest in a topic before it is reached in the curriculum. Teachers must be familiar with overall objectives so they can depart from a given sequence and capitalize on student motivation. Children are motivated to learn about familiar material. For example, we know familiarity helps students organize and make sense out of written symbols. A child that knows about cars can produce words, sentences, and stories about cars. Language experience stories, sentence strips and labeling objects in the environment will assist in learning to read. Student-centered activities can be designed to capitalize on their interests and ability levels. Therefore, rather than following a specific set of lessons for a long vowel sound, the teacher might provide experiences that are related to the student's language abilities.

Learning to read is easier if students react to familiar words. As students work with familiar words they begin to abstract the complexities of reading. At the sixth grade reading level, students are often assigned stories in a basal reader, but the same story will not motivate every student - not all students have the same interests. They are, however, all required to read the same story. Effective teachers often allow students to read student-selected stories. That is, they may choose to ignore the basal stories and allow students to acquire and extend reading abilities by reading library books. Students may then recreate segments of the story in a number of different ways. Diagrams, posters, book jackets, and commericals are examples of exciting ways to share a book's content. Students are more likely to be motivated to read when they are involved in selection of topics.

Social studies instruction is another area that relies heavily on a single textbook, but the intent of social studies instruction should go beyond book content. Social studies can be concerned with helping students learn to inquire and solve social problems. Learning content may not be as important as learning the processes of acquiring and evaluating information necessary to solve social problems. A unit approach or individual and small group research projects are subjectively more motivating and successful. The teacher can assign a chapter about the Ural Mountains and require content mastery on a written test. A more subjective approach might be to assign topics related to the influence of mountains on man. Students would gather, interpret, and explain their findings. One sixth grade class investigated mountains and concentrated on the influence of mountains on people. Several students had visited mountains on vacations and other people in the community that had lived in mountain regions were interviewed. The students were required to make models of mountains, pictures of mountain lifestyles, and represent other aspects of adaptation to mountain environments. They collected, examined and applied the information - they did not memorize content just to pass a test. The process of using content to solve problems was learned and retained because students were involved in the learning process.

Personal Goals

Personal goals can also be developed objectively and subjectively. Personal attitudes about behavior and learning are generally included in the personal goals of the elementary school curriculum. Rewarding students for appropriate behavior and academic performance is an objective method used to enhance personal goals - students that are positively reinforced will be encouraged to repeat appropriate behavior. Academic success can also be reinforced. When students achieve academic competence academic motivation will increase. The teacher determines the academic performance criteria and reinforces success. Because success tends to produce more success, students experiencing success in personal and academic development will continue to profit from the school experience.

Self-discipline is another aspect of personal development. Self-discipline can also be developed objectively. Teachers begin by establishing rules for classroom behavior and sanction students for compliance or noncompliance. Students that are praised for appropriate behavior will be encouraged to generalize learned behaviors in related situations.

Personal goals also have a subjective dimension. Students are naturally motivated to organize and learn about their environment. A teacher may capitalize on this natural motivation to learn by providing learning experiences that build on the students' ability levels and interest areas. Students will enjoy school and learning when the experiences are productive and relevant.

Classroom discipline is a topic that frustrates many educators. Subjectively, the goal for self-discipline is achieved as the student assumes responsibility for behavior. Involving students in establishing classroom rules (that can be amended by students) is one method of involving students. They may also be involved in determining consequences for inappropriate behaviors. Through active involvement they are likely to become even more responsible for their own behavior. Rather than externally control students, teachers can help students learn to guide themselves. In a recent preschool experience college students were having difficulty getting students to make choices. The college professor suggested that the college students leave the classroom and observe the young children through a two way mirror. When the students and professor left the room the children began making their own choices. Additionally, the children were observed effectively resolving disagreements.

Social Goals

The social goals of cooperation, citizenship, and aesthetic appreciation also contain objective and subjective evaluation dimensions. Teachers can influence social development directly through objective, direct intervention. These same goals can be developed through the use of subjective, indirect techniques. For example, teaching students to cooperate with others may be directly taught and objectively evaluated. Teachers may establish classroom rules that specify appropriate and inappropriate cooperative behaviors. They can then carefully observe students and praise them when cooperative behaviors are demonstrated. Students might also be taught basic cooperative skills that gradually lead to more complex cooperative behaviors. Objective methods for teaching cooperation require that the teacher consistently reinforce appropriate behavior. For example, one teacher that effectively used a direct method for teaching cooperation listed classroom behaviors on the board. She started with one behavior the first day of school. She stated the behavior, cited examples, and then asked students to repeat the behavioral rule. During the day the teacher observed the students and quickly praised those who implemented the rule while redirecting those students who deviated from the rule. She easily kept count of the times each student made an error. When the students successfully had mastered the first rule the teacher added another rule. She continued to reinforce the previous rule as she directed students toward mastery of the second rule.

A more indirect, subjective approach for teaching cooperation requires the teacher to create a learning environment in which students are

101

actually allowed or required to work with others. As situations requiring students to cooperate are presented, the teacher allows students to settle disputes under teacher supervision. Only in more severe situations will the teacher intervene. Rather than count the number of infractions committed by individual students, the teacher observes each student during interaction situations and determines whether or not the student is exhibiting cooperative skills. Students needing more direction may be provided with opportunities to work on activities requiring freedom and also may be required to work with fewer students. Proponents of this method contend that students can learn to cooperate only by working with others and devising ways to settle their own disputes (sometimes with teacher consultation).

Citizenship, another social goal, can be encouraged in the same manner as cooperation. Directed, objective techniques require teachers to identify and specifically state the tenents of citizenship. Subjective, student-centered methods provide activities that help them learn citizenship concepts through experiential activities and actions with others. An objective evaluation of a student's citizenship would require the teacher to identify exact behaviors and knowledge necessary for their definition of citizenship. If knowledge of the three branches of the federal government is a necessary prerequisite for good citizenship, the teacher would ask students to state the three. A subjective approach would not place as much emphasis on the specific facts. Instead, teachers would provide opportunities for students to share, to represent one another, and to establish classroom rules. Citizenship knowledge can be taught directly or indirectly - the evaluation that is used will then be objective or subjective, depending on teacher emphasis.

Health/Physical Goals

Kinesthetic development, coordination, health skills, safety and coping skills are also part of

the elementary school curriculum. These goals,
like all others, can be taught directly and evaluated objectively. They can also be taught indirectly through experiential activities and evaluated subjectively.

The process of learning to throw a football
can be directly taught and objectively evaluated.
The teacher would determine the student's present
ability level. The teacher would then decide that
specific sequence of instructional activities must
follow. The student would be given instruction in
one specific skill at a time with the teacher
objectively determining whether or not each skill
is mastered before proceeding to the next.
Measures of success might include distance, finger
placement, wrist movement, follow through, or the
quality of the spiral.

A more indirect method of teaching this same
skill might require the teacher to give students a
football and allow them time to practice throwing
to one another. Students having difficulties might
approach the teacher or the teacher might offer a
suggestion. Students would be likely to learn how
to throw a football just as quickly without direct
instruction. The teacher would subjectively evaluate progress by observing and judging the students' enthusiasm for the activity.

The elementary school is entrusted with the
goal of helping students develop their health
habits and skills. The topic of dental hygiene
helps demonstrate how objective and subjective
instructional and evaluation methods can be used.
A teacher using directed instructional techniques
would identify the specific behaviors students will
learn. For example, if a teacher wanted students
to learn the importance of eating good foods he or
she might show a film or invite a dentist to speak.
After the film or presentation, the teacher would
review the specific material considered important.
An objective test could then be administered and
those doing well on the test would have demonstrated mastery.

A student-centered approach to instruction would allow students to develop appropriate skills with more activity oriented methods. One teacher gave students chocolate cookies. She then gave them popcorn and carrots to eat. They examined each other's teeth after each item was consumed. The cookies left the teeth black and the popcorn and carrots removed most of the cookie residue. The teacher then passed out toothbrushes and had students brush with a clean white brush. The students saw the toothbrushes turn dark from cookie particles that were still in the mouth. Finally dental floss was provided and students discovered how even more cookie particles could be removed. The teacher evaluated the experience simply by listening to the student comments and was able to assess student learning by their comments.

TEACHER/DISTRICT PHILOSOPHY OF LEARNING

The teacher and school district philosophy of the learning process is a third factor affecting instruction and evaluation. There should be a philosophical basis behind every teaching act, and this basis has direct influence on testing and evaluation.

An examination of your philosophy will help you clarify your thoughts about instruction and evaluation. Your philosophical position probably lies somewhere on the continuum in Figure 2. The continuum, entitled "The Controlling Influence in the Educational Process", allows you to identify your belief system. For example, if you believe that the teacher/environment/school have a significantly greater influence on the material the student learns, you are environment- ally oriented. If you believe the student has a greater impact on the nature of what is learned, you are more student oriented.

At one end of the continuum lies the philosophy placing primary importance on the environment

Figure 2

The Controlling Influence on the
Educational Process

/_____/

Teacher   Child
Environment   (Interests,
District   Abilities,
Curriculum   Motivation)

and sources external to the individual. This point
of view is often expressed in the vocabulary of
behaviorist theory. To a behaviorist all knowledge
and behaviors are induced, shaped and reinforced by
external forces. The individual is not a creative,
initiating agent. Individuals learn and acquire
behaviors only as they are cued and reinforced by
the social and physical environment.

At the opposite end of the continuum lies a
philosophical perspective centered on the individual who is viewed as an initiating agent in the
world. The individual has internal drives and
motivations that are difficult to measure, but are
assumed to exist. This is a phenomenological philosophy. Individuals develop internal mental processes that are not overtly observable and human
learning is an interaction between the individual
and the environment. Each individual responds dif-
ferently to environmental situations and produces
different effects on the environment. Learning is
looked at as both a quantitative, factual acquisition process as well as a qualitative, internal
processing event. The thinking abilities of a ten
year old are qualitatively different than those of
a six year old. The behavioristic approach is

105

teacher-directed. A phenomenological approach is student-centered with the teacher seriously considering the whole child in curriculum decisions.

Each philosophic approach has an impact on the instructional procedures, including evaluation. From a behavioristic perspective all knowledge is identifiable, sequential, and presented using teacher-directed methods - skills and information are presented, practiced, and reinforced. The task of the teacher is to determine what sequence of skills or information the student is to learn, present and reinforce the material, and evaluate the mastery of the material. The teacher, through this process, establishes knowledge, skills and behaviors while extinguishing undesirable behaviors.

Classrooms utilizing behavioristic principles are teacher-directed. That is educational decisions are derived from the teacher, curriculum, or both. The overt use of rewards strengthens behavior and can be in the form of verbal praise or the use of tokens. Examples of typical behavioristic instructional programming would be the use of teaching machines, the DISTAR reading program or token systems.

Evaluation of behavioristic programs is direct and objective, and the material is quantitative in nature. Evaluation is designed to determine the amount and extent to which the knowledge has been mastered. The behavioristic philosophy assumes that all individual behaviors, skills, and knowledge are measureable, thus testing for specific information is always possible. Testing is based on the specified objectives and there are few, if any, subjective considerations (at least for the behavioral purist).

The student-centered philosophy of phenomenology places importance on the material learned by the student as well as the subjective nature of people. Teachers plan instructional activites around the needs and interests of students and the instructional goals of the district. Students are expected to master stated objectives, concepts, and skills. However, the unique manner by which each student acquires and processes information is considered and evaluated. Beyond the acquisition of specific skills, each student's learning must be evaluated in subjective terms.

Evaluation from a phenomenological perspective is much more subjective. The teacher will be making objective determinations of content mastery and subjective inferences regarding development. This development includes internal motivation, self-concept, self-discipline, as well as enjoyment, appreciation, and involvement in a topic. Students have been shown to have different learning styles, therefore any evaluation should include subjective considerations of these stylistic differences.

A brief outline of difference between behavioristic and phenomonological philosophies is listed in Figure 3. As you examine these differences, consider the information presented in this section and reflect on your own belief system. While your philosophy will most likely be a mixture of the two philosophies, certain predispositions will dominate. Your philosophy of learning will affect the evaluation emphasis you rely on.

Figure 3

Behaviorism and Phenomenological Characteristics

Behavioral	Humanistic
Factual questions	Affective, complex questions
Environment respons- ible for child's language	Child and environment are responsible
Explicit success	Inferential success
No internal locus of control	Internal locus of control
Teacher-directed instruction	Child-centered instruction
Behavior is predicted	Behavior is not predictable
Emphasis on reality of child	Emphasis on child's poten- tial
The child and his world are objective	The child and his world are subjective
Children learn to transmit knowledge	Children integrate and generate information

SUMMARY

In the elementary school, the nature of developmental tasks requires teachers to help students develop cognitive and affective domains. The emphasis of the school goals and teacher philosophy have a dynamic impact on the nature and focus of the instructional process. The instructional process and philosophy guide the style of evaluation. Objective and subjective evaluation were discussed as each applied to certain educational goals. The next two chapters will present how objective and subjective evaluations are utilized for specific elementary subjects.

108

References and Selected Readings

Erikson, E. H. Childhood and Society. New York:
    Norton Publishing Company, 1967.

Glasser, William Reality Therapy. New York:
    Harper and Row, 1965.

Hymes, J. L. Teaching the Child Under Six. Second
    Edition. Columbus, Ohio: Charles E. Merrill
    Publishing Company, 1974.

Kaltsounis, Theodore Teaching Social Studies in
    the Elementary School. Englewood Cliffs,
    New Jersey: Prentice-Hall, 1979.

Labinowicz, Ed. The Piaget Primer. Melno Park,
    California: Addison-Wesley, 1980.

Piaget, Jean The Psychology of Intelligence.
    London: Routledge and Kegan Paul, 1950.

CHAPTER 7

EVALUATION OF ACADEMIC ELEMENTARY SUBJECT MATTER

"There is something better than
a test ....when the test is over."
-Douglas (Grade 3)

The objective and subjective nature of the elementary age student has been presented in earlier chapters. This chaper presents useful hints for evaluation within the subject matter areas of the elementary school.

READING:

Reading is one of the most important subjects in the elementary school curriculum. As much as one half of the primary grade student's day is devoted to reading and reading related instruction while the intermediate age student will devote an equally significant portion of the school day developing and extending reading skills. Evaluation practices will vary according to the grade level and achievement level of the child.

Technical Assessment

Reading is generally divided into four categories: word analysis, vocabulary development, reading comprehension, and word study skills. Students may be strong in one area of reading achievement and not as strong in another area. The teacher must decide the specific skills important for emphasis and determine the student's functional ability in each area. We want to include one word of caution at this point, the teacher must remember that variations in learning style will allow some students to compensate for weaknesses in one area, such as word analysis skills, because of strengths in the other areas. Therefore, knowledge of achievement level in each category will help the teacher plan for individual needs and facilitate development of an overall program of instruction.

Most teachers will use the students' previous basal text level as the major determiner in reading placement. Teachers also look at prior achievement and ability tests as a means of selecting the most appropriate placement level at the beginning of a new year. However, the well organized teacher will focus on each student's abilities in each of the four major reading categories and plan instruciton accordingly.

Non Technical Assessment

Teachers begin each school year making placement decisions. Test scores and information from the previous year is not the only source of information as new students often arrive well ahead of their records. A reliable assessment method is to ask the student to perform tasks representative of skills in each of the four reading categories. This usually can be accomplished during a short work session while other students are engaged in another task. The student's word attack skills can be determined by selecting an appropriate grade level reading book and having a short passage read. This process will allow the teacher to make an accurate estimate of the student's word attack skills and reading fluency. Additionally, the teacher can ask questions at the end of the passage and make a quick determination of the student's oral reading comprehension. The student's silent reading comprehension can be checked by providing a workbook or task sheet with accompanying questions. The word study skills and the vocabulary skills are less important for initial placement. However, if a teacher wants some idea of the student's word and vocabulary skill levels, the following procedures will work. Ask the student to locate a certain word in the dictionary using guide words. Provide a list of words and ask the student to place them in alphabetical order. Vocabulary skills can be determined by asking the student to identify words in a spelling book. A teacher also might ask the student to identify the meanings of different prefixes and suffixes. By using ideas such as

112

these the teacher can make a general assessment of a student's reading abilities for initial group placement. We would remind you to keep close track of the student's daily progress as a means of checking on the appropriateness of the placement.

Assessing Daily Work

A teacher should also evaluate skill acquisition on a daily basis. The teacher must know what skills are being emphasized in each lesson and check to ensure that skills are being learned. This can be done by looking over daily work, observing the students at work, and by frequent formative evaluations. Many of the reading texts used in the elementary school include periodic unit tests that can be very useful. Daily and intermediate assessment is helpful. This short term assessment/review procedure can be very individualized and time efficient, especially after the teacher becomes familiar with each student.

Assessing Attitudes Toward Reading

Another aspect of reading instruction that is extremely important and often overlooked is the student's attitude toward reading. We know that students who do well in reading tend to enjoy reading and those doing poorly dislike reading. Teachers concerned with improving the student reading ability should consider the importance of enhancing attitudes toward reading - an enthusiastic reading teacher can improve a student's attitude and ability. An excellent indicator of a student's reading attitude is the number of books read. The teacher may want to provide students with regular free reading time and observe students during the period. Interest in reading as well as the kinds of books read are indicators of student attitudes. The student that is not attentive to the task or quickly skims through books may have a poor concept of reading, while the student that enjoys reading might need more reading time and assistance in selecting additional interesting reading material.

Reading has both an objective, skill oriented dimension and a subjective, interest oriented dimension. Students that do well in reading reinforce the joy and pleasure of reading by reading more. Those who are encouraged to read will become more competent in the reading skill areas.

MATH/ARITHMETIC

Elementary school children are generally grouped by math ability within grade levels - students are assigned to math groups on the basis of their ability levels. The dominant mathematics ability considered in math placement is mathematical computation ability as teachers tend to examine only the correctness of solutions to problems. Other aspects of math that need consideration include understanding of math concepts (can the student perform the correct operation at the appropriate time) and problem solving abilities (can the student use mathematical skills to solve problems). Assessment of each math ability is again both objective and subjective. Effective skill evaluation for grouping purposes requires more than simple comparisons of percentile scores, etc.

Teacher Made Tests

Initial evaluation should be deferred until the student has had an opportunity to review material learned the previous year. Teachers can then construct their own tests that include the major concepts and processes covered during the previous year. In many instances teacher-made tests can be more useful than past achievement test results. The teacher-made tests can also be used to help the teacher decide the skills that need to be emphasized and the skills that can be quickly reviewed. Emphasizing addition facts rather than proceeding to a more challenging concept may bore more capable students and contribute to a poor attitude toward math. Likewise, the teacher who overlooks a student's need for basic skill review by proceeding too rapidly or not providing sufficient review is going to produce enormous frustration for the low ability student.

Right or Wrong

The very nature of mathematics as a subject may lead the teacher in the wrong direction concerning student evaluations. By focusing on right and wrong answers the teacher may overlook the cause of the errors. For example, a student may not master division, not because he or she does not understand the process, but because one of the steps in the process has been forgotten. Renaming fractions provides another example. The student might be dividing the numerator and denominator by different factors. The error is procedural, not conceptual, so rather than evaluating the work as poor, the careful diagnostician can remediate the one specific problem. Math evaluation must go beyond objective scoring - teachers must examine the specific nature of each type of problem and not always rely on evaluation based on total percent correct.

Learning Rate

The individual learning syle and motivational level of the student are important diagnostic dimensions when considering math ability and progress. A fifth grade student may begin a unit on long division, do very well initially, and then become a behavior problem. When asked about his behavior, he states that he understood the process, was bored with division, and saw no need to do repetitive daily work. The teacher had not monitored the student's daily progress and had misinterpreted the cause of the misbehavior. The teacher finally decided to move the student to the next objective.

A group of sixth grade students were beginning to exhibit behavioral problems in a math class early in the second semester. The teacher had been drilling the students on their multiplication

115

facts and refused to proceed to division until the facts had been mastered. When the teacher decided to issue fact sheets and begin division instruction the behavior problems disappeared. When the students were asked why they thought their behavior had improved they stated that they were doing something they needed to know for seventh grade. The multiplication facts were still necessary, but by adapting the needs of the curriculum to the needs of the students the teacher was meeting the needs of both - the students were learning division and the teacher was allowing students to use the multiplication facts in a practical application setting.

The teacher needs to be alert to the different learning styles and needs of individual students. We have taught very gifted children that made numerous errors in the daily work as well as on tests. However, when we would sit with the students and ask them to solve specific problems, these students solved the problems quickly and accurately. Gifted students need subjective evaluation of their work and abilities. An over-emphasis on correctness and neatness may discourage their attitude toward math and affect their progress in math. For the very bright students, success may require a brief lesson or introduction, a limited amount of practice, experiences that apply and extend the principles of the lesson, and a brief evaluation. (This principle can apply to students other than gifted---the teacher must know the students and the teaching objectives.)

SCIENCE

The evaluation of science is both objective and subjective. The objective function of science evaluation deals with assessment of a student's demonstration of understanding. Most science programs utilize a term referred to as operationally defining a concept or procedure (an operational definitionis the scientific counterpart of a behavioral objective). An operational definition states what the student is to define or demonstrate and the acceptable criteria for performance. Operational definitions fit nicely with science because of the physcial interaction characteristic of scientific investigation. A young student might operationally define a magnet as a rectangular shaped piece of metal that picks up paper clips while an older student might define hydrogen as an invisible gas that will make a glowing splinter of wood pop (or explode). The teacher can readily determine the extent of student learning through the regular use of operational definitions - a process that includes both objective and subjective evaluation.

More subjectively, however, teachers can determine the students' scientific knowledge through observation. Some students are remarkably adept at involving themselves with scientific tasks. For example, most students marvel at the incubation and hatching of eggs. The interest and understanding can be inferred from the kinds of questions asked, the amount of enthusiasm they expressed towards the unit, and the kinds of comments teachers overhear as students work with one another. Using the example of an embryology unit, one teacher asked class members to explain the development of the eggs to students in other classes and the teacher could easily evaluate their understanding with no formal test.

Science is a subject that should encourage students to interact with their world, and the ten basic interactive scientific processes are identified in Figure 1. Because of the nature of child growth and development, several of the processes are appropriate for early primary grade students and others are more appropriate for the students in late concrete operations or early formal operational thought. Teachers can evaluate the students' understanding of the different processes by providing them with experiences and activities requiring utilization and development of each process. Therefore, evaluation must be based on observations of students as they interact with objects and materials.

117

Students that have had a good science back-
ground in the preschool and primary grades tend to
read better and tend to be better problem solvers.
The kind of program beneficial at the preschool and
primary level cannot, of course, be content
oriented. At this level students need real experiences with "things" from their immediate environment and need to be encouraged to develop their
powers of observation and classification. They are
learning how to collect and organize information -
the same processes used in reading and mathematical
problem solving activities. This cannot be taught
from a book and it cannot be omitted by teachers
simply because they feel intimidated by science.
The best science lessons are those that involve
objects of interest to the students and allow them
to manipulate and discuss what they have manipu-
lated. Therefore, evaluation should be more subjective.

Science in the elementary school serves two
functions: to expand the students' understanding of
the physcial environment and to develop their
understanding of the scientific processes. Evaluation of science ability should not rely solely on
content acquisition. Science instruction and evaluation must go beyond the content of science books
and provide students with hands-on experiences that
encourage the manipulation of objects, examine how
objects and materials can be altered through their
actions on them, and provide them with opportunities to gain both a sense of respect for, and
mastery of, their world. Instruction based solely
on content and evaluation of facts does not go far
enough in developing the students' scientific abilities, therefore objective evaluation is not as
appropriate as subjective evaluation.

Figure 1

Scientific Processes

Process	Grade Level	Description
Observing	Primary-Intermediate	Using five senses to gather information including noting attributes and parts.
Classifying	Primary-Intermediate	Organizing material and ideas into groups with similar characteristics. Noting similarities and differences.
Space/Time Relationships	Primary-Intermediate	Past, present and future; position in space such as right, left, up, down, front, back; determining how objects fit together and can be disassembled, etc., and shapes.
Using Numbers	Primary-Intermediate	Numbering objects, ordering quantities, relationships between quantities (more and less) combining and separating quantities, etc.
Measuring	Primary-Intermediate	Comparing and describing physical attributes and relationships in increasing standardized means.
Communicating	Primary-Intermediate	Use of oral and written language as well as graphs, maps, and diagrams to represent information.
Predicting	Primary-Intermediate	Suggesting what will happen under given circumstances.

Inferring	Mid-Primary-Intermediate	Suggesting reasons for an occurrance, explaining an observation.
Controlling Variables	Intermediate	Understanding factors affecting an action of out-come and altering factors to change or test the pos-sibility of an outcome.
Interpret-ing Data	Intermediate	Reaching a conclusion based on data and using processes of inferring, predicting and making conclusions.
Formulat-ing Hypotheses	Intermediate	Making generalizations based on observations and information that apply to related situations and events.
Defining Operation-ally	Intermediate	Describing or giving an understandable meaning to an object, event, concept or procedure by explaining the action that will pro-duce a desired result or the consequence of the action.

SOCIAL STUDIES EVALUTION

Social studies instruction has experienced changes similar to science and math evaluation. In the past teachers relied on large, beautiful social studies books that contained color pictures and well organized chapters. Each chapter had a title and subtitles, important content (the capital of the Belgian Congo, Columbus discovering the Americas, etc.), and objective evaluations at the end of each chapter. The traditional approach to

120

social studies was teacher-directed and content-based. Students were evaluated on their ability to read, recite, and test.

More recent approaches to social studies instruction emphasize the importance of concepts (rather than facts) and student inquiry (rather than read-recite). Teachers are being encouraged to develop social studies teaching units that incorporate map and globe skills, content that supports concept development, and consideration of student personal and social growth. Rather than utilizing a single basic social studies text, teachers are encouraged to use a variety of resources supporting teaching units.

Evaluation of the social studies must change as the instructional empahsis changes. Because basic content is not regarded as important as concept instruction and inquiry, teachers can not evaluate social studies knowledge by simply asking objective questions. A typical social studies unit plan should include the concepts, skills and objectives to be learned by the students. A portion of the evaluation may be objective such as asking students to list five reasons for Russia being a world power or six Christmas customs we have adopted from other countries. But evaluation must also be subjective. For example, students may demonstrate an understanding of the concept of compromise by developing rules for their own games, setting up an island government, or solving a behavioral conflict between two students in the classroom.

Social studies instruction should also feature interactive opportunities. That is, students should be allowed and encouraged to interact with one another on group tasks. One teacher, studying the American Revolution, asked students to form groups and investigate certain aspects of revolutionary life. One group examined living conditions, another studied methods of warfare, another studied colonial trade. Rather than prepare written reports, each group was to make a collage that

121

demonstrated those specific aspects of colonial life. The teacher evaluated the students' work subjectively in two areas. The first area involved the extent to which the products revealed student knowledge and understanding. The second examined the kinds of social interaction that had taken place as students worked together in groups. The teacher identified the leaders, the workers, the encouragers, and those who needed encouragement. This information was every bit as useful as the product evaluation. The teacher had the opportunity to see how students worked and solved problems together.

Another responsibility of the teacher is to ensure that each student has an opportunity to develop positive, personal self-esteem. This means that timid, unliked students have a chance to interact with others in a positive setting. One method of facilitating this social development is by using prescriptive seating arrangements. A sociogram can be very useful for teachers as they obtain information for rearranging seating assignments. The teacher asks students the names of five children they would like to invite to a party. The lists are examined to determine which students might benefit from each other. The teacher can then place two relatively shy students next to one another knowing that they have a positive regard for each other.

WRITING EVALUATION

Writing instruction can be separated into two dimensions - writing skills and content. Writing skills include the mechanics of writing such as punctuation, capitalization, tense, usage, and parts of speech. Writing content includes the more styalisticaspects of the writing process - meaning, main idea and organization. There are three types of content writing: elicitive, informative and expressive. Each type of writing has a different purpose and students should have experience with each type. As discussed earlier, the emphasis of writing has shifted away from an emphasis on creative writing toward an emphasis on skill acquisition. Both aspects are important and both need to be included in elementary school instruction and evaluation. Elicitive writing is directed at the ability to request or call for action and it directs the writer to persuade others, informative writing involves the student in reporting factual information and conveying knowledge, and expressive writing includes those writing assignments referred to as creative writing in which the student conveys imagination and feelings. Examples of elicitive writing include attempts to persuade a parent into a certain course of action or writing a member of Congress persuading him or her to vote a certain way. An example of informative writing would be a written book conference or an itenerary of a student's vacation. Examples of expressive writing include asking the student to write about three wishes, favorite food, or a description of the most horrible monster imaginable.

Evaluation of this type of writing must include the nature of the assignment and the extent to which the intent of the assignment is met. The teacher also should evaluate the appropriateness of the assignment in terms of the audience to which the writing is addressed. Because there is a lack of objective material, evaluation must be of a comparitive, subjective nature. The inexperienced teacher will have a more limited concept of the appropriateness of the written work, but must still make evaluations based on what is known about the student and what is known about the abilities of other students. The intelligent teacher also will maintain a collection of each student's written work and evaluate the writing progress in terms of the improvement made by each student. Teachers, parents, and students can understand improvement when recent work is compared to previous work.

Evaluation of specific writing skills is much like evaluation of reading and math skills. The teacher may rely on achievement test scores as well as test found at the end of units in the English books or other textbooks. Teachers may also elect to construct their own evaluations for analysis of specific skills. One teacher, after presenting a unit on capitalization skills, wrote several nonsense sentences on the board excluding the appropriate capitalization. Students were instructed to correct the sentences and then construct examples of their own. This exemplifies teacher-constructed evaluation that is often more effective than standardized achievement test results because the teacher is measuring skills in which the students have received instruction.

Teacher-made evaluations are just as appropriate in evaluation of other writing skills. The teacher that has just presented instruction in correct noun-verb agreement might require students to correct examples developed by the teacher. While teachers can evaluate specific objectives in this manner, they can also examine the extent to which students apply newly acquired skills in their other written work. The teacher evaluating noun-verb agreement would be wise to examine written stories to determine whether or not the students are applying specific skills beyond the paper-pencil test.

References and Selected Readings

Harris, Albert J. (Ed) Casebook on Reading Disability. New York: David McKay Company, 1970.

Kane, Robert B., Byrne, Mary Ann, and Hater, Mary Ann. Helping Children Read Mathematics. New York: American Book Company, 1974.

Mayhew, Lewis B. "Measurement of Noncognitive Objectives in Social Studies," in Harry D. Berg (ed.) Evaluation in Social Studies, 35th Yearbook of the National Council for the Social Studies. Washington, D.C.: National Council for the Social Studies, 1965.

Miller, William C. "Unobtrusive Measures Can Help
    in Assessing Growth," Educational Leadership
    35: 264-269, January 1978.

Pflaum, Susan. The Development of Language and
    Reading in Young Children. Columbus, Ohio:
    Charles E. Merrill Company, 1978.

Smith, Frank Comprehension and Reading, New
    York: Holt, Rinehart and Winston, 1975.

CHAPTER 8

EVALUATING NON-ACADEMIC AND SPECIAL AREAS

"Tests are to see if you learned
anything since the last test.
They are really good if you get
95%." -Troy (Grade 5)

The previous chapter presented strategies for evaluation in the academic areas. We emphasized both subjective and objective approaches. This chapter presents strategies for evaluation in the following non-academic areas: art, music, physical education, personal and social development, and the special learning needs of children.

ART EVALUATION

Approaches to the organization and evaluation of art experiences follow from the phenomenological and behavioral views of human development. The phenomenological philosophy argues that the student has a unique inner self that can be creatively expressed. Self evaluation provides opportunities for the student to examine his or her representations of inner ideas and feelings. A behaviorist would dismiss this premise because they do not theoretically acknowledge an inner self. The behaviorist looks at the change in human behavior only from a quantitative external perspective. Thus, the behaviorist considers free expression as an inappropriate method of developing artistic abilities. The behaviorist would view art products from a knowledge and skill perspective that can be systematically developed and objectively measured.

These divergent positions have influenced approaches to art instruction and evaluation. Art, like other subjects, includes affective and cognitive dimensions and may be evaluated through subjective and objective approaches. Traditionally, art education has emphasized the affective input and subjective analysis of the art experience.

127

Some school districts, however, are attempting to identify and implement an art education program with a prescribed scope and sequence. This scope and sequence design identifies goals, objectives, and prescribes specific areas for objective teacher evaluation. This section presents useful information related to subjective and objective art evaluation procedures.

Art has traditionally been the elementary school subject that encourages affective expression. Students need opportunities to reflect and express their feelings, emotions, and creative thoughts through artistic representations. Teachers, believing that art experiences should reflect personal feelings, have not evaluated the student art products in terms of objective artistic skill. Subjective evaluation has been used as a means to gain unobtrusive insights. Teachers have been able to extend their knowledge and understanding of students by examining the content of their art work.

Cooperative teacher-student evaluation of art work may encourage the student to identify areas for further skill development. The teacher might visit with the student and ask questions such as: "What are you trying to express?", "How well do you think you have done?", and "What might you do to improve the picture?" This type of teacher-student analysis allows the student to evaluate his or her own work, identify areas of difficulty and methods for improvement. It also provides an excellent opportunity for the teacher to encourage continued skill development.

There are art educators and psychologists that support art skill development through teacher-directed methods. Teachers identify specific skills, teach the skills to students, and provide appropriate practice. They believe that art skills can be taught to students in such a way as to help them better express themselves.

Many students begin to lose interest in art during the upper elementary years. Interest is lost because students cannot demonstrate the skills necessary for adequate expression. Teachers can identify objectives that will help students extend artistic skills, and progress can be measured objectively.

Typically, objectives of elementary art instruction can be categorized into four elements of art. Figure 1 identifies and provides examples of these elements.

Figure 1

Elements of Art

Elements	Examples
Design	Objective repetition, objective placement, shape, texture, line, and color.
Color	Primary, secondary, and tertiary colors; value; tints; and tones.
Perspective	Overlapping, size and placement of objects, horizontal and vertical placement, size and distance, brightness and distance.
Figure Drawing	Body proportions, representing the body, placement of facial features.

The above categories can assist in the organization of objective art evaluation. Teachers can evaluate student progress on each element by first identifying the area of emphasis and then evaluating their instructional and motivational effectiveness through student art products.

Perhaps one of the most difficult problems facing art teachers is to determine the appropriate balance between direct instruction and creative expression. While creative expression is an important goal, many students lose interest when they realize that their skills are not maturing. Teachers can continue to enhance artistic development by providing helpful hints and instruction in a well-organized, sequenced program that provides for both creative expression and non-threatening evaluation.

Evaluation of art skills does not require normative comparison. Teachers can evaluate individual student progress by measuring the student growth according to each specific element. Evaluation with an individual emphasis requires the teacher to collect art samples for the purpose of measuring progress. Regardless of a subjective or objective approach to art instruction and evaluation, the student's art work should not be measured against absolute standards nor the work of other students.

PHYSICAL EDUCATION

The major reason for evaluation in physical education contexts is to determine how effective the experience has been in enhancing the physical and emotional development of the student. Thus, the focus of evaluation can be on the psychomotor outcome of the physical education experience or the focus can be on the skills acquired through the process of physical education.

In elementary schools physical education experiences range from nonstructured recess experiences to organized skill-oriented programs with physical and attitudinal objectives. Our experience suggests that the latter is the most rewarding for elementary students. We also believe that while skill development is critical, attitudinal concerns must be considered. Evaluation of individual progress in physical education usually occur in the categories of physical development, attitudes, skills, and program quality and both objective and subjective strategies can be used. However, the classroom teacher will be evaluating primarily in the subjective domain. Does the student look forward to phsical education? If not, then is there something the classroom teacher can do to provide a more positive attitude? The student who is constantly forgetting a gym suit, etc., or the child who makes excuses to avoid participation may have an attitudinal problem. Additional ways of assessing attitude include observations, anecdotal records, teacher student conferences, diaries, or autobiographies.

The most positive physical education experiences are those in which students gain in physical skill and competence, peer approval, and in a sense of the importance of physical activity for lifelong health. The classroom teacher can enhance these areas by being subjectively aware of students' attitude about physical education.

MUSIC

Elementary music programs include a series of skills, knowledge, and attitudes designed to develop students' musical potential, creative expresiion, and aesthetic appreciation. Music, unlike other subjects in the elementary school, has few tangible products; the songs students sing are seldom recorded and therefore unavailable for later reflective evaluation. Occasionally music teachers administer paper and pencil skill tests, but the majority of instructional time is allotted for vocal production.

You, as a classroom teacher, are unlikely to have the training necessary for professional subjective analysis. Likewise, because of limited musical training, you are unlikely to be familiar with the scope and sequence of skills within the music curriculum. But, rather than avoid music,

131

you should incorporate musical experiences into your own instructional units. At the same time you will also be in a position of supporting and reinforcing the work of your school's music teacher. Your evaluation needs must therefore be concerned with the effectiveness of musical experiences in the lives of students and should focus on their enthusiasm as they participate. For example, students in one class were studying a region of the United States. During a formal music class students sang folk songs from that region. When they returned to their regular classroom teacher they expressed enthusiasm towards the songs from the region and the teacher added the songs to the next day's social studies lesson. The teacher evaluated the experience several ways. First, students were observed tapping desks in time with the music. Secondly, many students whistled the tunes during recess. Additionally, they kept requesting time to practice and asked if their parents could be invited to listen. Finally, the teacher considered the positive comments made by parents when the parents did visit.

Unfortunately, too many negative evaluations may decrease the students' participation and interest in music. Students mature at different rates and classroom teachers should use music experiences that do not adversely affect those students developing more slowly. The classroom teacher has the responsibility of maintaining a positive attitude toward music and using interesting music experiences to enhance instruction in other areas. Thus, the regular classroom teacher should evaluate students from the affective perspective.

EVALUATING SOCIAL DEVELOPMENT

The students' social development reflects the acquisition of interaction skills and students must develop appropriate skills for interacting with other students and adults. Evaluation of social development must be comparative and personal. The

132

social expectations and skills of the first grade
student differ from those of the sixth grade student and these differences require unique evaluation procedures. Teachers can make fairly reliable
evaluations of the students' social abilities within the classroom context because the natural comparisons of behavior allow teachers to assess the
social abilities of each child. This comparative,
normative approach will enable the teacher to identify students with strong, average and weak social
skills. Students with problems will need to have
specific behaviors documented so that the teacher can
identify specific weaknesses and substantiate subjective evaluations.

A checklist can be useful in this situation.
The teacher identifies the areas to be observed and
evaluated and then records student social skills.
Figure 2 is an example of a possible checklist format with suggested categories for evaluaton.

Figure 2

Checklist of Social Skills

Skill	Strong	Ade-quate	Needs Improvement

Cooperates with other children:
  1:1
  small groups
  large groups			

Participates in:
  small groups
  large groups			

Respects:
  rights of others
  property of others
  feelings of others			

Uses appropriate language
  accepts criticism
  good sportsmanship
  shares materials and
    teacher time			

The students' personal-social development must be carefully observed by the teacher. The students' ability to become self-disciplined is perhaps the most critical personal-social skill and the teacher is responsible for creating a classroom environment that will encourage them to develop self-discipline. Even the inexperienced teacher can identify those students that cause problems in the classroom - but the inexperienced teacher usually do s not know what to do because the specific nature of the problem is difficult to define. When a discipline problem emerges the teacher needs to begin observing and objectively recording information about each incident. Figure 3 illustrates a typical documentation form that can be used to record observable student behavior. The teacher records each incident and, after enough data has been recorded, analyzes the behavior relative to the time and individuals involved.

Figure 3

Documentation Form

Date	Time	Setting	Behavior	Action Taken

The teacher now has objective data from which to draw conclusions and form a plan of action. In one class eight students were observed out of their seats during math class. Closer analysis (after several incidents) revealed that this was right after recess. Rather than modify the students' behavior, the teacher decided to alter her behavior and decded to read for a few minutes following each recess period. Another example revealed that whenever a certain boy and girl were seated near one another during spelling, they would cause problems for one another. The teacher showed the data on the documentation form to the two students and they decided to sit apart during spelling class.

Too often inexperienced as well as experienced teachers operate from a basis of insecurity and guilt. If a student is a problem in the classroom the teacher considers the problem as a reflection on his or her teaching effectiveness. The fact is, however, that these students have had their entire lives to develop these behaviors and that these behaviors did not emerge as the result of one teacher (usually). Therefore, teachers need to enlist the help of their principals and the parents whenever they consider extra support beneficial. The parents and principal can be shown the documentation form and allowed to make their own conclusions regarding the student's behavior. The teacher has the information in a professional presentation that parents and administrators can not dismiss. The only course of action left is to support you.

Teachers are responsible for informing parents about other aspects of students' personal development. The checklist in Figure 4 includes personal traits that affect student classroom behavior. Teachers can use such a checklist to make comparisons between students, develop a student profile, and to determine personal traits needing more attention.

Figure 4

Checklist For Personal Development

Traits	Strong	Adequate	Weak
Sense of humor			
Blame acceptance			
Confidence (self-assured)			
Works independently			
Makes accomplishments			
Task oriented			
Need for frequent rein- forcement			
Completes work on time/ responsible			
Patience			

IDENTIFICATION OF CHILDREN WITH SPECIAL NEEDS

PL 94-142, "The Education of All Handicapped Children Act", requires schools to identify handicapped children and educate them in the least restrictive environment. While formal evaluation is necessary in the identification process, the classroom teacher is instrumental in initial identification of children with possible special needs. Formal evaluation procedures are conducted by professionals with specialized training, but the classroom teacher is the professional charged with the responsibility of referring children with special needs. This section outlines pupil qualities and traits that teachers can look for as they interact with children on a daily basis. These ideas do not necessarily mean that any child with one of the traits is exceptional, only that a child may have special instructional needs.

136

This section briefly summarizes traits and behaviors that may be indicative of learning deficiencies or exceptionalities in the following areas: learning disabilities, speech handicaps, mental deficiences, visual and auditory handicaps, and behavioral disorders. Intellectual giftedness is also an exceptionality. Traits of gifted children will also be discussed in this section.

Learning Disabilities

Children with learning disabilities are not children with low mental abilities. A learning disabled child usually has average or above average ability, but is not achieving at or near the expected ability level. Usually the learning disabled child has difficulty learning by traditional school methods and requires special or additional instruction. The causes of learning disabilities are uncertain, but due to either perceptual, maturational or processing difficulties, the child is unable to achieve at the expected ability level. Children not diagnosed may fail in school, become behavior problems, and eventually give up on their educational pursuits. Children with learning disabilities are now more fortunate because of the increasing availability of information, ideas, and teaching methodologies.

Children with learning disabilities may exhibit several identifying characteristics. Learning disabled children often achieve two grade levels below their ability level in one or more academic area. Teachers should compare student achievement and intelligence tests in order to identify students with possible learning disabilities. A child's capacity for auditory and visual memory also may be indicative of a learning disability. A child with limited auditory memory (ability to remember what is heard) may be unable to hold or remember items long enough to mentally process the information. The same is true for a child with weak visual memory skills. The child may see the material

137

but be unable to remember the information long enough to process it mentally. Learning disabled children quite often exhibit reversals in spelling, writing, and reading. The infamous "b and d" reversal is frequently observed in the writing of all children but the learning disabled child will continue to exhibit these and other reversals much longer than normal. Reversals in reading also may be observed. A child might read the word "was" for "saw". Disabilities may also be detected in the child's reading. The child may omit portions of a word, substitute letters or prefixes/suffixes, or combine letters from one word in the sentence with letters from another word on the same or a parallel sentence.

Art work may also indicate a learning disability. The child with an inability to represent body proportions relative to other children the same age may indicate perceptual problems and a learning disability. Mixed dominance such as a right-handed child that is left-footed or relies on the left eye may reflect a learning disability. Additionally, the teacher may observe poor coordination or excessive difficulty processing information.

These are only a few indicators of children with learning disabilities. The teacher is reminded that these are only indicators and the teacher observing any of these indications should refer the child to a trained diagnostician for more formal assessment.

Speech Handicaps

Speech teachers traditionally have focused on enunciation and articulation difficulties. Recently, however, their scope and function have changed. Today speech clinicians are becoming involved in problems children have with encoding, processing, decoding, and producing language. The classroom teacher needs to be able to identify children with possible articulation

problems as well as children having difficulty
with grammar, syntax, and semantics.

While the area of speech diagnosis and cor-
rection is quite specialized, the classroom
teacher needs to be aware of advances in the
speech clinicians' duties and indicators useful
in screening. Articulation and speech production
problems that extend well beyond normal maturational development should be referred to the
specialists. Also, the child that is having
extensive difficulty with oral sentence construction and word order needs to be referred.
Finally, the child that has difficulty retrieving
information and the child that takes much too
long grasping for an internal idea may need
referral.

Mental Deficiencies

Mental deficiencies usually are synonymous
with mental retardation. The regular classroom
teacher may easily detect children with low mental abilities by observing the quality of work
and the quantity of work. Children with very low
abilities have difficulty grasping many academic
concepts and are behind other children in personal care skills. Should you as a teacher sus-
pect a child of having an extremely low mental
aptitude, you should refer that child for formal
testing. Be careful, however, not to label a
child too early or assume that slower children
are mentally deficient. Many slower children
have unique learning styles or may be matura-
tionally behind....not mentally deficient.

Visual and Auditory Handicaps

Generally, the child that can not hear or
see is identified before entering school. However, the classroom teacher will need to be aware
of possible problems in these areas in the event
that a child begins to loose either of these
faculties. Young children also have problems
with fluid in their ears which may affect their

hearing ability. Parents are often not aware of subtle changes in the child nor aware that a child with less than normal acquity has a problem. As teachers work with children, they should be alert to these types of problems. Then, as with most other problems, an appropriate referral should be made.

Behavior Disorders

Behavioral disorders usually do not go unnoticed as other handicaps or disorders might - behavior disorders are easily observed in most classrooms. Behavior must be defined in terms of what is appropriate for children at a certain age, and children with marked deviations exhibit behavioral problems. Disorders most commonly encountered and discussed in the schools are those in which children are too aggressive or overt. But there are other types of disorders that the teacher needs to be aware of. Some children are the opposite of the "typical" behavior problem, and they tend to withdraw or show lack of interest. Other behavioral disorders affect the child's personality. Children that are shy, easily frustrated, anxious, or self-conscious also may have problems. The following checklist (Figure 5) includes different behavior areas. The teacher needs to be aware of these types of problems as he or she interacts with the children.

Figure 5

Behavioral Checklist

Name_____

Item	Strong	OK	Weak	Comments
Aggressive				
Disobedient				
Bully				
Tantrums				
Negative				
Uncooperative				
Uninvolved				
Shy				
Self-confidence				
Frustration level				
Self-conscious				
Daydreams				
Lazy				
Interest level				
Hyperactivity				

Gifted

While gifted children are not considered handicapped in traditional terms, they do have special needs. Many states are requiring schools to identify gifted children and provide appropriate experiences for their needs. The gifted child may be classified in a number of ways, depending on the criteria established by the state or school district. Often children with IQ's of 125 or 130 and higher are classified as gifted, and children with IQ's of 140 and above are classified as highly gifted. Ordinarily one might assume that identification of gifted children is easy - one need only to look at the child's group IQ test to determine the IQ or look for children with consistently excellent work. While these methods are effective in many instances, many children do poorly on group IQ tests and may not do well on daily work. An alert teacher may need to examine other traits that indicate giftedness such as those suggested in Figure 6.

Figure 6

Selected Characteristics of Gifted Students

Sense of humor	Dominating personality
Excellent reasoning	Divergent thinking
Excellent judgement	Poor penmanship
Inventive	Bored with routine
Novel Solutions/ideas	Elaborative thinking
Sense of wonder	Risk taking
Curious	Excellent achievement
Spontaneous/impulsive	Verbal fluency
Intuitive problem solving	Social interactions
Independent	Alert observer
Organizer	

Teachers need to identify gifted and creative students in order to meet their specific needs. However, teachers are usually accurate less than 50 percent of the time. Careful attention to traits such as those outlined in Figure 6 should improve the successful identification rate.

References and Selected Readings

Bailey, R. A. and Burton, E. C. The Dynamic Self. St. Louis: C. V. Mosby Company, 1981.

Blankenship, C. and Lilly, M. S. Mainstreaming Students with Learning and Behavior Problems. New York: Holt, Rinehart and Winston, 1981.

Edwards, Betty. Drawing on the Right Side of the Brain. Los Angeles: J.P. Tarcher, Inc. 1979.

Kirk, Samual A. and Gallagher, James J. Educating
     Exceptional Children, Third Edition. Boston:
     Houghton Mifflin Company, 1979.

Powell,   Marcene L. Assessment and Management of
     Developmental Changes and Problems in Chil-
     dren, Second Edition. St. Louis: C. V. Mosby
     Company, 1981.

Van Osdol, William R. and Shane, Don G. An Intro-
     duction to Exceptional Children, Second Edi-
     tion. Dubuque, Iowa: Wm. C. Brown Company,
     1974.

CHAPTER 9

REPORTING STUDENT PROGRESS

"The teacher never called my
parents yet. But if she did,
my mother would tell me and I
would run to my room and lock
the door." -Tracy (Grade 6)

The focus of this chapter is two fold. We
want to suggest approrpriate strategies for evaluating student achievement and we want to recommend useful methods for conferencing with and
reporting progress to parents. The methods used
by teachers to evaluate student achievement are
one of the most criticized dimensions of the
teacher's responsiblity. The habits and customs
of teacherparent conferencing are among the most
primitive and archaic of school interactions.
Each of these areas needs immediate improvement if
we are to establish credibility with the students
we teach and the parents with whom we interact.

SPECIFIC EVALUATION CONCERNS

The number one source of student anxiety in
school is fear of failure, and grades are the primary focal point. The number one source of a low
academic self-concept is academic evaluation. The
grading of student work can reduce anxiety and
encourage positive academic self-concept development if used correctly. This can be accomplished
through a teacher's committment to one basic
belief - grading should be diagnostic and prescriptive.

Numbers and Letters

The grade at the top of a paper should tell
the student what was right or wrong with the paper
or project, it should not appear as though the
grade came out of thin air and mystically landed
on the top of the page. I remember getting a
grade of B-C+/B on a theme. It was a format I was
unfamiliar with and the grades themselves were

meaningless. I did not know what I had done wrong nor did I have any idea how to improve in order to receive a higher grade the next time. Similarly, a simple ninety percent on an art project with no explanation or recommendations is useless. The excellent classroom teacher should make a professional committment to diagnostic and prescriptive evaluation so that grading is not a magically devised number. Examine the instructional value in the following theme evaluation methods (Figures 1-3).

Figure 1

Letter Method

A-/C+

Figure 2

Analytic Method

	Possible Pts.	Pts. Received
Creativity	5	4
Organization	5	4
Vocabulary	5	5
Spelling	5	3
Grammar	5	2
Total	25	18

$25\overline{)18.}$ = .72 = 72%

Figure 3

Rating Method

Poor	Weak	Ave.	Good	Excellent
1	2	3	4	5

Quality of ideas	1 2 3 4 5		x 5 =
Organization	1 2 3 4 5	sub	weight
Style, Flavor,	1 2 3 4 5		x 3 =
Wording	1 2 3 4 5	sub	weight
Grammar	1 2 3 4 5		
Punctuation	1 2 3 4 5		
Spelling	1 2 3 4 5		x 1 =
Legibility	1 2 3 4 5	sub	weight

The letter method in Figure 1 offers no diagnostic
or prescriptive information – areas for improvement
are left completely to the student to determine.
The analytic method (Figure 2) tells the student the
valued criteria and the instructor's assessment of
performance on the criteria. The student can
readily see that grammar and spelling need improvement. The rating method (Figure 3) is the most
elaborate method and it is also the most instructionally effective. The criteria are expressed with
weights emphasizing the intent and focus of the
particular assignment. A dittoed evaluation sheet
could be returned to students along with the essay
or theme for ready reference during a teacher/stu-
dent follow-up conference.

<u>Computing the Grade</u>

Reporting forms will always be with us. They
may take several different forms, but they will
always be included as part of the teacher's responsibility. Record keeping is absolutely necessary for
effective summative reporting and the methods of

record keeping will determine the accuracy and effectiveness of final reporting. Daily grades, homework grades, participation grades, and test grades all contribute to the final grades. The accuracy of these grades and the accuracy of their computation will affect the validity of the final grades. The following suggestions may assist you in the preparation of final grades.

Do Not Average Letters

An average devised from an A, B, and C, seems easy enough to compute. It is a B because the A and C cancel. But what about more complicated combinations such as A, B-, C+, D, A, C, and F. This may be compounded because different exercises may have had different importance. Get the picture?

Do Not Average Letters and Numbers

Assume that your grade book includes the following homework grades for Suzie: A; 87; C; 92; B+; 78; and 82. It would be difficult to assign a percentage grade because you can not assign a percentile value for the A, C, and B+. In a situation such as this you can either make a subjective appraisal of Suzie's work and not assign a letter grade.

Use Numbers Whenever Possible

A smiley face on the top of a paper may mean something to a third grader, but try averaging seven smiley faces, two frowns, and one catatonic expression. We can perform numerous mathematical computations with numbers. Percentages can be calculated, weights can be assigned, and rankings can be determined. We suggest the use of numbers whenever you are attempting to determine percentile type grades.

Use Checklists for Evaluating Processes

Percentile grades are not always necessary. For example, if a student has to successfully

complete seven steps to do a good book report then
list the seven steps and check completion of each
step. You may even want to rate the performance of
each step. Furthermore, if you want to evaluate a
student's tennis serve, a checklist might be just
the tool you need.

	Excellent	Average	Needs Improvement
Stance			
Grip			
Toss			
Follow-through			

This type of analysis helps the student and
teacher determine where the problem is with this
student's serve. The student is assisted by the
evaluation and the teacher looks more competent.

REPORTING TO PARENTS

Because of the nature and importance of
reporting student progress, teachers need to ensure
that the reporting process, either written or personal conference, is an effective, honest appraisal
of a student's efforts and progress. A successful
conference is one in which appropriate information
and feelings are shared objectively and subjectively, thus helping create a stronger, more positive bond between home and school. Parents better
understand the goals and methods of the school,
develop a trust towards the teacher, and become more
responsive to teacher requests for assistance at
home.

Parents have a significant impact on the student's school achievement, even a greater effect
than schools have. Thus, they should always know
the level of their child's performance so they can
monitor the progress and provide assistance. Schools

149

have traditionally informed parents of student progress through the use of report cards. More recently however, a trend of systematically combining parent-teacher conferences with grade reports has emerged as a method for advising parents about student progress. Parent-teacher conferences allow the teacher to communicate directly with the parents and can reduce misunderstanding. They also serve as a medium for orienting the parents to the philosophy and nature of instruction in the school.

Hopefully, you will be reading this chapter well before conferencing and reporting time so you can begin to organize yourself for a successful conference. This chapter also should help the new and the experienced teacher appear knowledgeable and organized. We hope to help decrease the amount of anxiety experienced by conferencing and help you plan a more positive conference. The following suggestions are based on the experiences of successful teachers and should help you conduct excellent parent-teacher conferences.

Be Cool

Before embarking on an explanation of other hints for effective conferencing, a word of encouragement might be in order. Parents have a remarkable propensity for seeing their own personal traits in their children. This means that parents have a personal commitment to their children and are emotionally involved when discussing important aspects of the child's behavior and educational progress. Parents may get upset easily, and, like their children, quickly try to shift the blame or rationalize inappropriate behavior or unacceptable progress. The experienced teacher, expecting a certain amount of avoidance behavior, should decide to listen attentively, paraphrase the parents' statements, indicate understanding, and offer insight - not judgement. If the topic is too extensive for one conference, you may schedule a more detailed follow-up conference after you have had time to assess the parents' claims. What the teacher must avoid during a conference is a confrontation. Parents may express unsubstantiated feelings or opinions that the teacher is not prepared to respond to. Simply listen and ask for suggestions. Parents are not often as objective as a teacher and approach conferences expecting to hear the worst. As you approach a conference remember that the parent is probably as nervous as you.

Emphasize Skills Not Grades

Effective education is reflected in successful programs and by teachers who have well defined goals and objectives. These goals and objectives become the medium for effectively evaluating students as an organized instructional sequence complements evaluation. Too often teachers plan conferences around achievement test scores and unit/chapter test scores. These scores have little meaning to the parents as they rarely are familiar with the material contained in the test or unit. As elementary teachers, we grouped students according to ability level for reading instruction. I would conference with parents of all students in my homeroom, even those students that went to another teacher for reading instruction. The other reading teachers would provide me with material to support their written comments about a student's reading progress. Usually, several of the statements were of no use or meaningless to the parents. Consider the following statement: "Carl is reading in book 3 and doing fine. At times he needs extra encouragement to complete his work. The last test revealed a weakness in word attack skills. At this time his progress is satisfactory." How many parents know what is contained in book 3, what word attack skills are, and how a student needing extra encouragement and a weakness in word attack skills can be functioning at a satisfactory level? Parents need to be shown the skills being taught and the relationship between skill performance and test scores. This will help them understand the complexity of the progress report.

151

Accentuate the Positive

An excellent way to begin a conference is by discussing the student's strengths. Parents will become more comfortable and relaxed if conferences begin with a positive note. Later, when the student's problem areas are discussed, the parents may be less defensive and more confident that the teacher has a total view of their child. As parents become more comfortable they may disclose statements such as, "I was weak in math too." Because the parents have relaxed and become more involved in the conference they are more ameanable to discussion about skill deficiencies. The antagonism that sometimes characterizes a parent-teacher conference may be lessened because parents realize that they are talking to a teacher who really cares about their child. Therefore, we suggest that you begin your conference by discussing positive aspects about the student, even if it means discussing the student's interests and efforts in certain areas.

Be Specific About Areas That Need Attention

Be specific. That is, discuss specific skills and competencies rather than general grades. Parents want to know how they can help, and they can help their child practice skills at home. You can enlist parent support and they can complement your instruction and lend their influence to enhance skill development. Organize every conference so the conference begins with a discussion about the student's good points. Then proceed to areas of difficulty. Finally, as elaborated in a later portion of this chapter, devise a plan for remediating specific problem areas. The conference is not complete if the parent leaves with little hope for the child's improvement.

Share Examples of Student Work

Do not save everything for the conference; children in the elementary school should take work home on a regular basis. Many teachers begin the

152

year by constructing individual student folders so that examples of the student's work may be cataloged until conference time. An introductory art activity might even allow the student to decorate his or her folder. By doing this you will inform students about two things: the teacher will conference with parents and some work will be saved for the conference.

Work placed in student folders should not be haphazardly selected. Teachers placing items in folders with little or no consideration for the quality and content may cause confusion when the examples they share with parents contradict the teacher's evaluation. Samples of student work should reflect their best attempts on specific skills selected for instruction. One method for obtaining examples of their best work is to inform students when specific assignments will be saved and placed in conference folders. The students also should be told the exact nature of the assignment as well as the criteria the teacher will use for evaluation. This will help ensure that children are in fact concentrating on the skills being evaluated and that they will be doing better work. This work may then be more representative of their true abilities than work with little effort. At the time of the conference the teacher will then have examples that reinforce the teacher's evalution.

Organize Before the Parent Arrives

As a teacher you have undoubtedly experienced those situations when you had not prepared yourself for a particular lesson and got lost or contradicted yourself in the middle of the lesson. A conference that is not well planned is like a poorly planned lesson: it will result in contradictions. Nothing is more awkward than not knowing what to say or saying the wrong thing. The poorly planned conference also wastes the valuable time you have with each particular parent. Both the teacher and the parent will be disappointed at the conclusion of a poorly planned conference.

The efficient use of time is important in each conference. Proper organization and planning should include consideration of the important topics needing consideration for each student. You should decide which topics are important and which topics may be omitted for each student. The inexperienced teacher may spend too much time on the unimportant topics or be diverted by parent small-talk and not have enough time to discuss the important aspects of a student's progress. For example, one teacher became very frustrated with the conferencing procedure. She felt that she had gotten to know the parents well and covered reading progress quite well, but she wasn't addressing the problems certain students had in other subjects. She decided to omit detailed reading evaluation for students doing well in reading and "personalize" conferences to the needs of each student. Once you have determined the important issues for each conference you may want to arrange the supporting material to correlate with your presentation.

Conferences Should Be Dialogues Not Monologues

The purpose of parent-teacher conferencing is to encourage parent-teacher interaction and discussion of student progress. Stop periodically during the conference and allow the parents to contribute. You may need to ask several questions to stimulate discussion. For example: "Do you feel I am accurate in my assessment? Does your child act this way at home? Have other teachers reported this finding to you?" Additionally, allow and encourage parents to ask questions about each area evaluated. Actively solicit their perceptions and questions.

Quite often parents will not respond when asked if they have any questions. The teacher must be a keen observer during the conference. Do not feel that because there were no questions that the conference went well. Parents may be apprehensive and tense during the conference and therefore reluctant to express their concerns. As you conference, establish eye contact with the parent and look

154

for signs of concern. If the parent seems particularly nervous during a portion of the conference or when you detect signs of uncertainty, stop and ask the parent to share specific concerns. Your attention to their feelings may turn an apprehensive conference into a cooperative, sharing experience. Furthermore, when people are nervous or anxious they do not listen: they talk or think about their own concerns. You are in charge of the conference so it is your responsibility to make people feel more relaxed and comfortable - look for signs of uncertainty and encourage parent input.

Schedule Conferences Like a Professional

Teachers that plan too many conferences in a limited time-frame will antagonize waiting parents and allow too little time for effective conferencing. Generally, twenty or twenty-five minutes are adequate for normal conferences. But, if you anticipate the need for a longer conference, you should plan for more time. The following suggestions will help ensure that parents are provided enough time and that the time will not be wasted.

1. Plan enough time

You will have easy and difficult conferences so you will need to plan the amount of time well in advance. In helping you plan enough time you may decide to alternate difficult and easy conferences. In this way difficult conferences can be given more time. We have also found it necessary to schedule "open times" to allow time to relax and to provide a cushion for conferences that are exceptionally long. The impression you make with your schedule will carry over to the substance of your diagnosis and prescription. A positive impression makes you appear more professional and more believable.

155

2. Consider parents' schedules

Scheduling conferences is difficult. Teachers usually send conference notices home. Times are scheduled and spaces are provided for alternative times. This becomes a difficult task to manage because most parents will not be able to attend at the scheduled time and you will need to readjust the entire schedule. Telephoning parents is an excellent alternative - it may require extra effort initially, but it will be a more efficient use of your time. Call the parents and arrange a mutually agreeable time over the phone. You may be able to synchronize conferences with other teachers and save extra visits for parents with several children in your school. Working parents appreciate conferences during days off or non-working hours and you can easily arrange such visits using the telephone.

3. Send reminders

The confusion during conference time may result in forgotten conference appointments - either the teacher or the parent may be at the right place but have the wrong time. By sending a reminder home the day before the scheduled conference you can remind parents and double check your own schedule. The awkwardness of waiting for a parent can be reduced by systematically reminding parents.

Have Suggestions Prepared in Advance

Little good is accomplished when the teacher evaluates a student poorly and has nothing to offer in the way of help. If a student has a problem the teacher must have some idea for improvement, and parents can often help. A student with problems in a specific academic area may benefit from extra work with the parents. You should have specific tasks and materials for the parents to use as they work with their child. You should also caution the parents to keep the practice session low key and enjoyable. One attempt to enlist parent help backfired. A teacher had asked a parent to help the child improve spelling skills by practicing a list of 1,000 words. Within a week the child was complaining to the teacher because the overzealous parent had the child working on 100 words a week. If done correctly, the student receives two benefits from extra parental help. First, the student receives specific help in needed skill areas. Secondly, the student has a period of time when he or she has the complete attention of the parent. The interaction between the child and parent can strengthen the child's attitude toward school as well as the parent's attitude toward education. Parents often feel helpless about their child's education. Suggestions from the teacher will make the conference more positive and give the parent direction in helping the child.

Interpret Standardized Test Scores

This topic may require some homework because it will be to your advantage to understand and interpret standardized test scores. Schools committed to involving parents in the educational process usually share achievement and IQ test results with parents as a matter of policy. Teachers should begin explaining test results by first explaining the scope and accuracy of the test results. For example, parents should know that tests often include material not covered in school, are given in a group setting, and provide general indications of student progress in relation to other students. The parents also should be informed about the method of reporting results. Generally, test results are reported in percentiles, stanines, and grade equivalents, each based on a raw score, student age, and grade placement. The teacher should emphasize the relationship between standardized test scores and the student's school performance. If test results are available from previous years, the teacher might also compare recent test results with earlier results. Patterns of underachievement may emerge and be meaningful for diagnosis and prescription. For example, an analysis of Amy's previous scores revealed that her achievement had dropped steadily on three successive achievement tests. The parents had been concerned about her behavior at home and the teacher was concerned about her school progress. The conference ended with the teacher and parent agreeing to a referral to the school psychologist.

Look For Solutions Not Blame

The conference is not a guilt seeking nor a blame placing process. The intent of the conference is to share perceptions of the student, report progress, and examine alternative solutions. Be careful not to accept the blame for a student's weakness or failure and do not cross-examine the parents to see if they are to blame. Psychoanalysts are trained to locate blame - teachers and parents are not psychoanalysts. Your job is to seek solutions that both you and the parent can implement.

SUMMARY

It has been our experience that teacher evaluation and grade reporting habits as well as individual conferencing styles mirror instructional organization. The teacher who teaches from an instructional plan that features instructional and terminal objectives tends to have organized instructional presentations. Similarly, this same teacher's evaluation format and grading practices usually are equally well organized because grade reporting and conferencing are systematic processes. You can create an impression of competence and professionalism by conducting organized, informative conferences.

References and Selected Readings

Bailard, V. and Strong, R. Parent-Teacher Confer-
    ences. McGraw-Hill, 1964.

Berger, E. H. Parents as Partners in Education.
    St. Louis: C. V. Mosby Company, 1981.

Bigner, Jerry J. Parent-Child Relations. New York:
    MacMillan Publishing Company, 1979.

Brandt, Ron S. Partners: Parents and Schools.
    Alexandria, Virginia: Assotiation for Super-
    vision and Curriculum Development, 1979.

Gordon, Ira J. and Breivogel, W. Building Effective
    Home-School Relationships. Boston: Allyn and
    Bacon, 1976.

Kroth, R. L. and Simpson, R. L. Parent Conferences
    as a Teaching Strategy. Denver: Love Publish-
    ing Company, 1975.